THE SHORT NEWS

SEAN ROMERO

Sky Pony Press
New York

To my wife, Maria: for believing in me and this project, encouraging my toy purchases, and very patiently photoshopping dust out of every picture in this book.

First Edition

Sky Pony Press books may be purchased in bulk at special discounts for sales promotion, corporate gifts, fund-raising, or educational purposes. Special editions can also be created to specifications. For details, contact the Special Sales Department, Sky Pony Press, 307 West 36th Street, 11th Floor, New York, NY 10018 or info@skyhorsepublishing.com.

Sky Pony® is a registered trademark of Skyhorse Publishing, Inc.®, a Delaware corporation. Books, authors, and more at skyponypressblog.com

Visit our website at www.skyponypress.com.

10 9 8 7 6 5 4 3 2 1

Library of Congress Cataloging-in-Publication Data is available on file.

Cover design by Kate Gartner
Cover photo by Sean Romero

Print ISBN: 978-1-5107-3738-9
Ebook ISBN: 978-1-5107-3743-3

Printed in China

TABLE OF CONTENTS

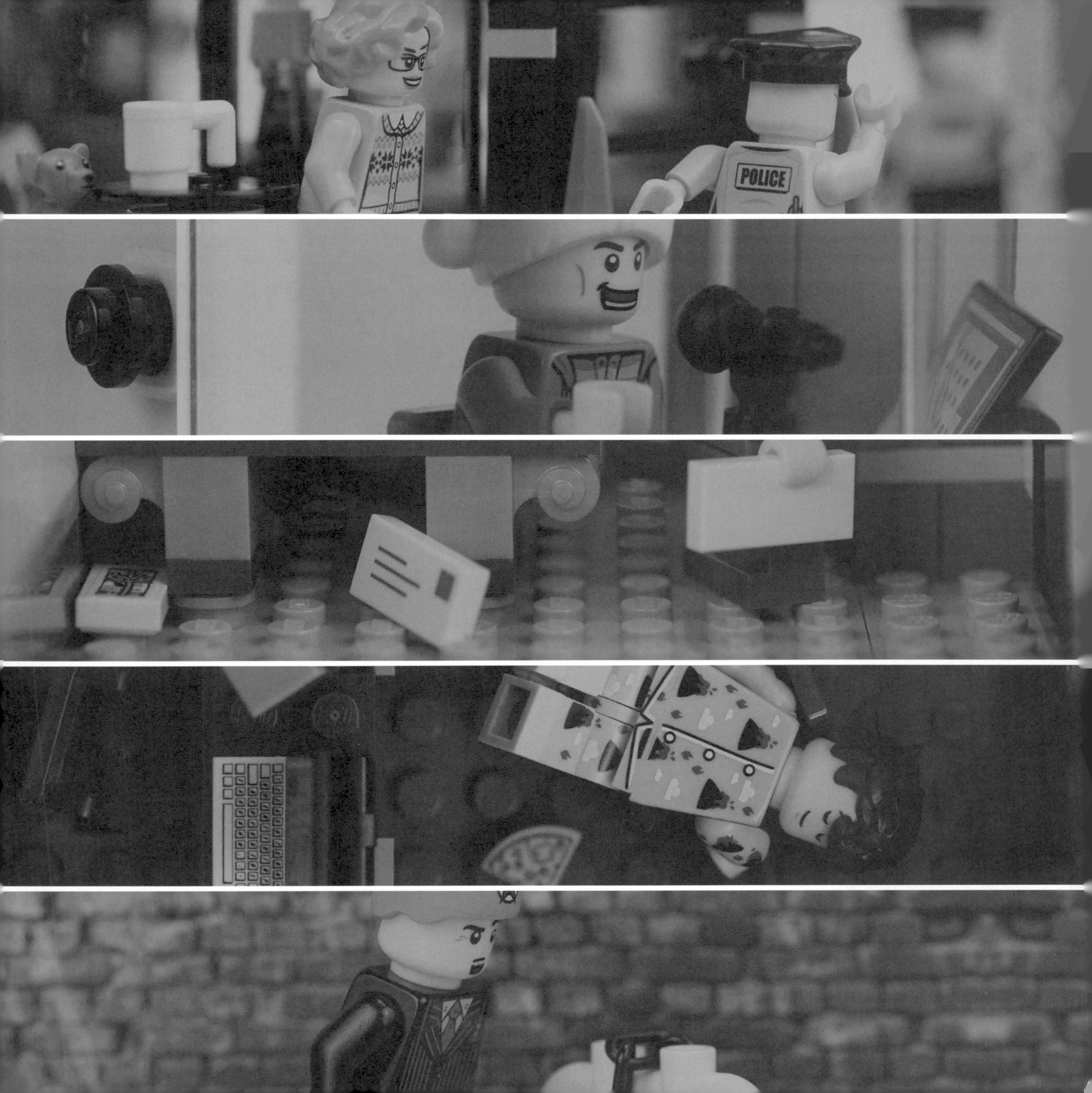
POLICE

CHAPTER 1
JOBS AND SIDE JOBS

PLANE FULL OF PLUMBERS FORCED TO LAND BECAUSE OF TOILET PROBLEMS

A Norwegian Air Shuttle flight was forced to return to Oslo because of toilet problems, even though there were more than eighty plumbers on the flight!

Just minutes after take-off, the flight to a trade event in Munich, Germany was abandoned when a crew member noticed a problem with the toilets. The announcement was met with laughter, with one passenger (a plumbing company CEO) later stating that the plumbers would have liked to fix the restrooms, but it had to be done from the outside and they didn't want to risk sending a plumber to work at over 30,000 feet! Following the announcement, the plane had to circle in the air until it was light enough to land. Thankfully, nobody needed to use the bathroom during this time!

COP CHASES HIMSELF FOR 20 MINUTES

An undercover police officer chased himself for twenty minutes after a CCTV operator mistook him for a suspect "acting suspiciously."

The junior officer from Sussex Police was on patrol when he received information about the "suspect" from a CCTV operator, who proceeded to direct the officer's pursuit. As the officer and suspect were the same man, they were constantly running in and out of alleyways at the same time. Despite the near-misses, the officer was reassured by the operator that he was "hot on the heels" of the suspect. The mistake was identified twenty minutes later when a sergeant passed by the CCTV control room and recognized the officer. Details of the blunder were leaked to *Police* magazine, but naturally, Sussex police did not provide any further information.

Dude, where's my bicycle?

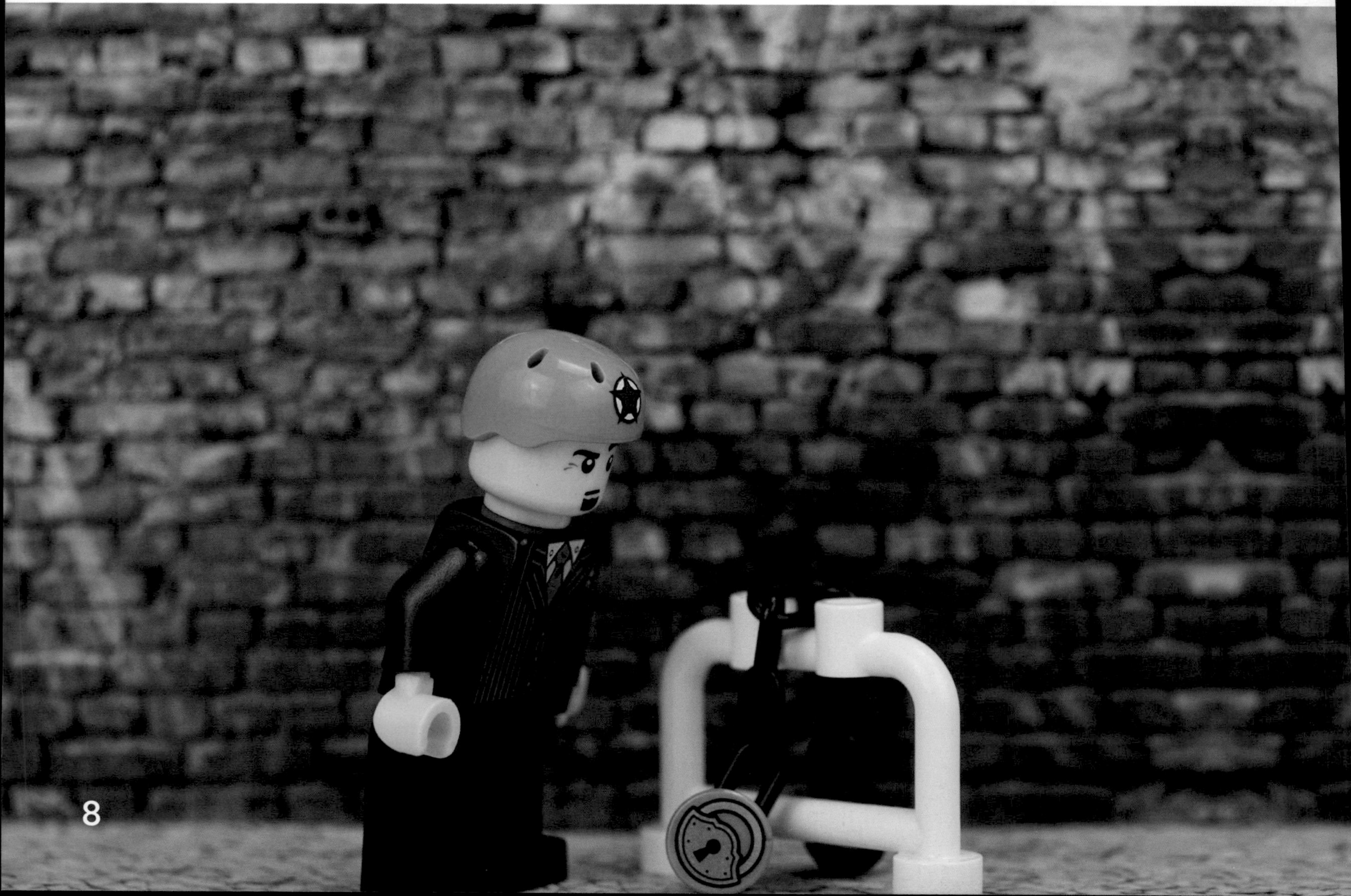

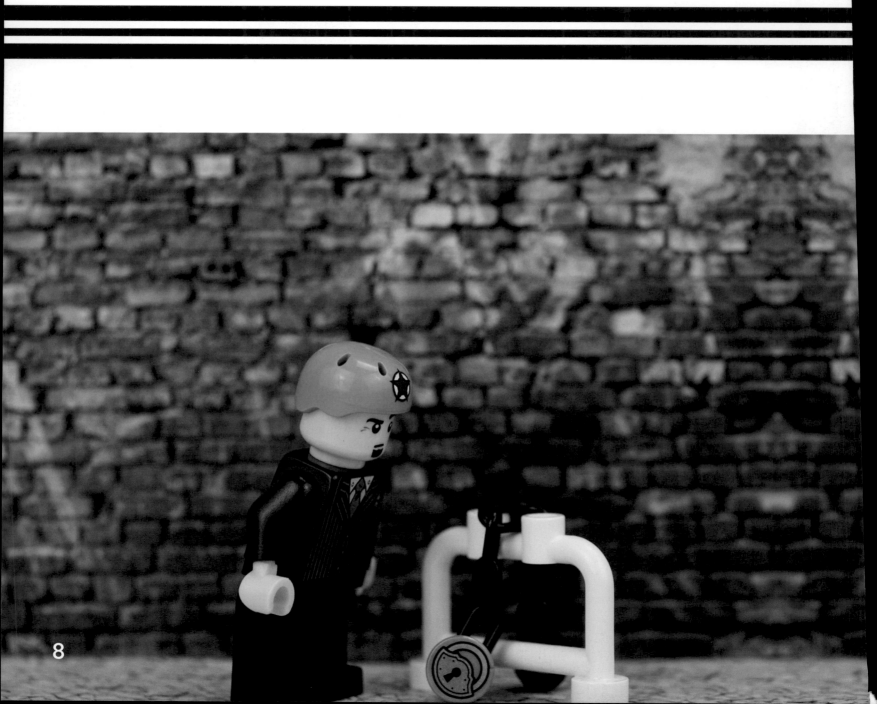

A Belgian Minister who rode his bicycle to a conference to promote cycling found out it was stolen in the half hour that he was away!

In his role as minister for mobility for Flanders, Ben Weyts discussed a plan to invest over $3.5 million dollars into bicycle lanes until 2019. The proposal was part of a plan to promote alternative modes of transport, given that Belgium has some of the worst road congestion in Europe. According to a spokesperson for the Minister, the bike was locked in a rack at the station, but it was not there when they returned. Ben had to arrange for his driver to pick him up from the station. It was hoped that security footage would help to locate the thief.

MAN SOLD HIS HOME AND SLEPT AT WORK

A Rhode Island city employee sold his house, so he did what anyone else would have done—he set up a makeshift bedroom at work, complete with a bed, nightstand, and coffee maker!

It's reported that the bedroom was located on the second floor of the Cranston Highway Department building. A photo of the bedroom showed pajamas on the bed and a pair of slippers on the floor. City Administration Director Robert Coupe made little comment on this matter, other than to confirm that the unnamed employee had been disciplined. This is a classic case of sleeping on the job vs. sleeping AT the job!

EL "FUNCIONARIO FANTASMA"

A Spanish man who hadn't turned up to work for six years was caught when his boss tried to present him with an award for twenty years of service!

Joaquin Garcia's job was to supervise the construction of a waste water treatment plant. His boss thought he was being supervised by local authorities, while the Deputy Mayor believed Garcia's boss supervised him daily. Everything unraveled when his boss tried to give him a plaque for twenty years' service. It was reported that Garcia claimed he went into the office, but those close to him said he dedicated his time to reading philosophy. The Spanish media dubbed Garcia el "funcionario fantasma" (i.e. "the Phantom Official"). Garcia was fined around $35,000, a little less than his gross $45,000 annual salary.

DJ PLAYED WHAM'S "LAST CHRISTMAS" TWENTY-FOUR TIMES IN A ROW

An Austrian DJ locked himself in his studio and played Wham's "Last Christmas" on repeat twenty-four times in an ordeal that lasted nearly two hours.

Joe Kohlhofer from radio station Antennae Carinthia refused to let other staff in the studio and told his co-host he would be doing the morning show on his own. Joe told his listeners that he felt people were not getting sufficiently into the Christmas spirit and that he planned to rectify that by playing "Last Christmas" for his entire two-hour slot. Joe received numerous calls to end the pain caused by the 1984 hit, but only yielded when his four-year-old daughter called and asked him to stop. The station says the stunt was not sanctioned and that Joe would be disciplined.

PEOPLE PAY TO STROKE BEARDS

A UK business offered bearded men the opportunity to earn forty dollars per hour just for having their beards stroked in a shopping center!

The world's first beard-stroking station was aimed at helping stressed shoppers unwind at the mall. The theory is that warm touches between humans release oxytocin, which is the hormone that reduces levels of the stress hormone, cortisol (much like stroking cat fur). Customers were invited to register online beforehand, with sessions of ten or twenty minutes. Customers were provided with music, oils, and water, tea, or coffee. The station was operated by Mo Bro's at the Highcross Shopping Centre in Leicester.

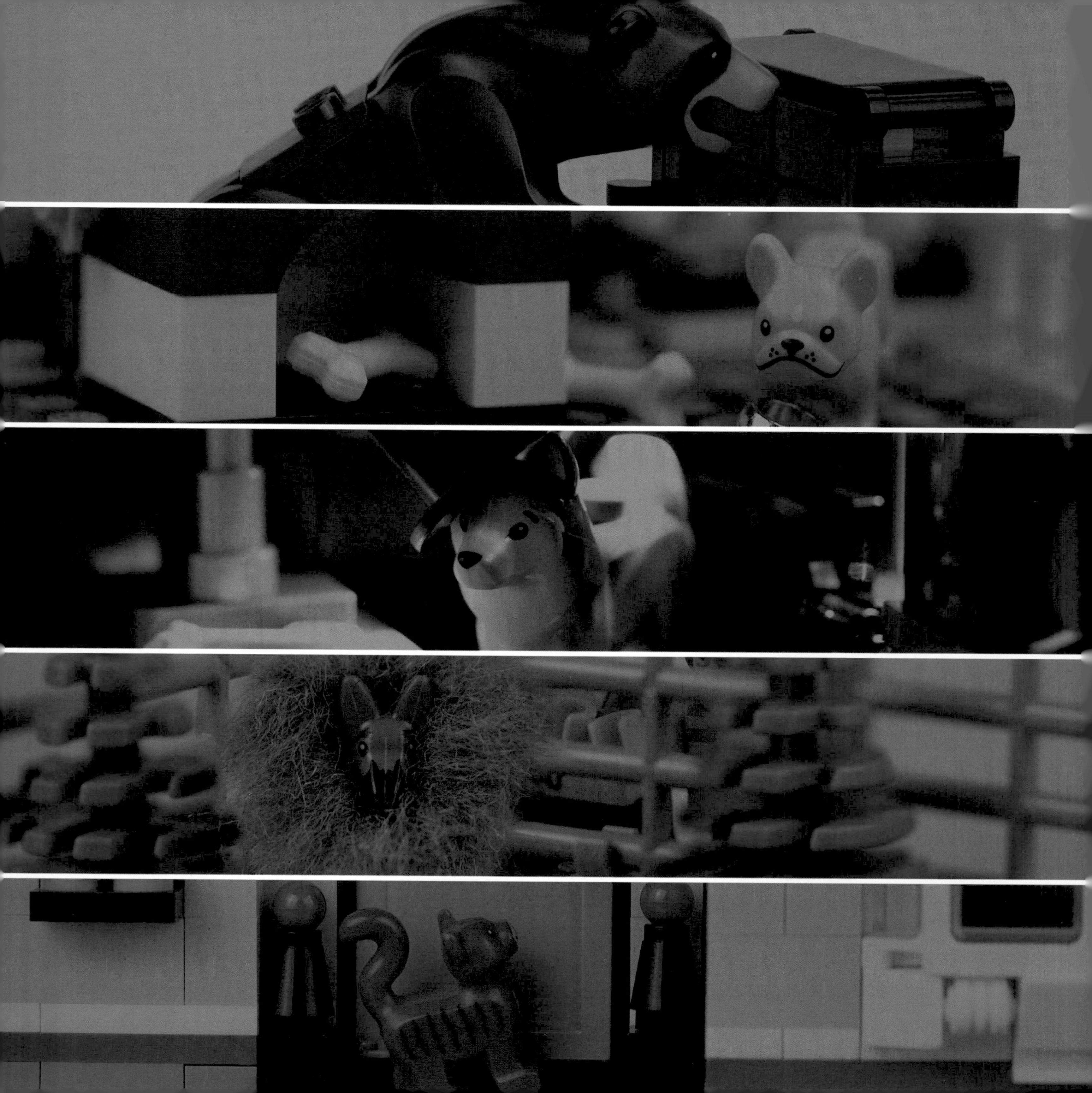

CHAPTER 2
ANIMALS

TWO DOGS TAKE THEIR OWNER'S TRUCK FOR A JOYRIDE

Two dogs in Tulsa, Oklahoma caused traffic mayhem when they took their owner's pickup truck for a joyride and crashed it into a river!

Roscoe and Luna (a Border Collie and a Labrador) had been left unattended by their owner "Scott" in his truck, which was parked on a hill. When one of the dogs managed to put the truck into gear, it rolled three blocks down a four-lane highway, through a stop sign, and eventually crashed into the Arkansas River. Somehow, the runaway truck missed oncoming traffic and joggers. When the fire department arrived, they found the dogs but no driver, with Scott later saying he initially thought his truck had been towed. Roscoe and Luna were released without arrest, but Scott's truck did not fare so well.

DIAMONDS ARE A DOG'S BEST FRIEND

When Lois Matykowski lost her wedding ring, she turned her home upside down and searched her dog Tucker's poop for weeks, but was unable to locate the ring until Tucker coughed it up six years later!

At the time, Lois had been married for twenty years and Tucker was a four-year-old Rottweiler known as the "food burglar" in the house. Recently, Tucker swallowed an unattended popsicle (including the stick), which was coughed up after a visit to the vet. This must have been the catalyst, as Tucker became sick two days later and coughed up the missing wedding ring. Lois says she screamed when she cleaned up Tucker's vomit and found the ring, which had lost none of its sparkle after a clean.

Handsome gorilla melts hearts at the zoo

24

Women flocked to a Japanese zoo to catch a glimpse of Shabani, a handsome gorilla who has been dubbed *ikemen*, or "good-looking man" by the locals.

Shabani lives at Higashiyama Zoo and Botanical Gardens in Nagoya, where his handsome looks and dramatic poses have won him a legion of female fans. A zoo spokesperson says that Shabani rests his head on his chin and looks intently at visitors, with his paternal instincts and watchful eye a feature found to be attractive by many. Shabani weighs 400 pounds and is said to be more "buff" than most gorillas with "rippling muscles." Shabani was born in the Netherlands before being raised in the Sydney Taronga Zoo, then moving to Higashiyama.

DUKE THE DOG RE-ELECTED AS MAYOR

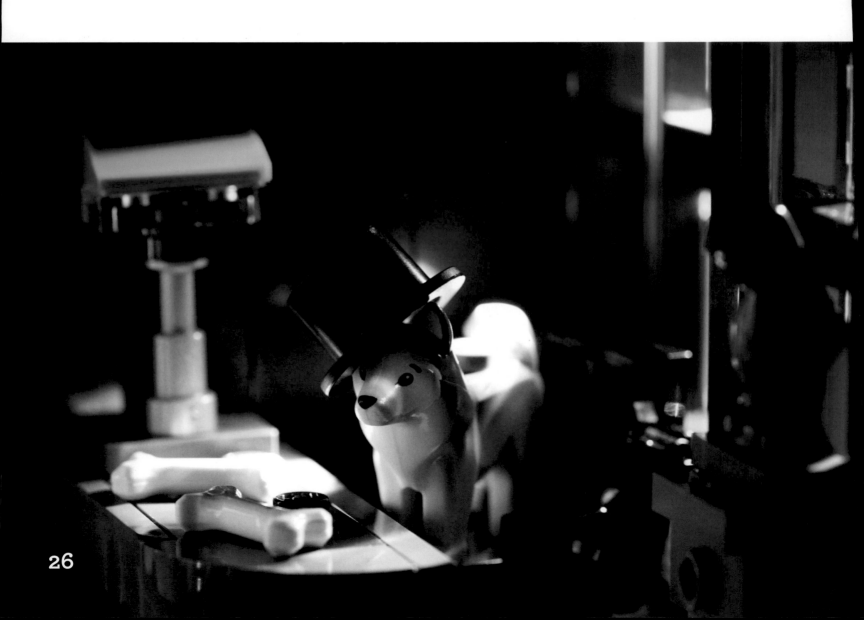

Duke the Dog must be a particularly good boy, as he was elected for a fourth term as Mayor of Cormorant Township, Minnesota!

Duke's owner David Rick says that Duke was accidentally voted into office for his first term, when only twelve votes were cast via write-in. Since then, Duke has really taken to his role with arguably the highest approval ratings in the country, his own Facebook page, and a feature in National Geographic! Local Karen Nelson told WDAY 6 that Duke has "done great things for the community," and doesn't know who'd run against him. While Mayor Duke does not draw a formal salary for his work, the townspeople treat him with belly scratches and food.

CHINESE ZOO TRIES TO PASS OFF DOG AS A LION

A zoo in Henan province, China tried to pass off a Tibetan Mastiff as an "African Lion," but the game was given away when the "lion" started to bark in front of visitors.

It's reported that the dog was placed in a cage labelled "African Lion" at the People's Park of Luohe after the real lion was temporarily sent to a breeding facility. While the Tibetan Mastiff is a particularly hairy breed of dog, pictures indicate that this wasn't a particularly convincing lion. Several visitors felt cheated by the $2.45 (fifteen yuan) they spent to see the animals at the zoo, complaining about the lion and other animals, such as a white fox in the leopard's den.

IN THEORY, SPIDERS COULD EAT EVERYONE IN A YEAR!

Great news fellow arachnophobes! There are so many spiders that, in theory, they could eat every single person on Earth in just one year!

According to data collected by European biologists Klaus Birkhofer and Martin Nyffeler, spiders eat "400-800 million metric tons of prey" every single year, including insects, birds, lizards and small mammals. As the estimated biomass of all humans on Earth is 357 million tons, spiders could eat everybody well before the end of one year. To make matters worse, a recent study carried out by Peer J revealed that 100 percent of homes in North Carolina contained spiders. Sure, the chances of a takeover are slim (if we're gone, who will spiders torment?), but they're not nil, either . . .

MICHAEL PHELPS RACES A CGI SHARK

Olympic champion swimmer Michael Phelps raced a simulated Great White Shark to kick off the Discovery Channel's Shark Week special, but lost the 100-metre race by two seconds.

Rather than race a real Great White Shark, Phelps was pitted against a computer-generated image of a shark, which swam a time consistent with the real-life speed of sharks. As Great White Sharks can easily reach speeds of twenty-five miles per hour (compared to humans' 5.5 miles per hour), Phelps was given some assistance with a wetsuit and monofin to mimic the shark's powerful tail. However, the twenty-eight-time Olympic medalist completed the race in 38.1 seconds, behind the time of 36.1 seconds clocked by the "shark." Phelps has called for a rematch in warmer water.

COME TO AUSTRALIA, WHERE IT RAINS SPIDERS!

Locals in Goulburn, Victoria claimed that "hundreds of little spiders" were falling from the sky and a "cotton-like substance" was covering their homes.

Chillingly, naturalist Martyn Robinson confirmed that such an event is explained by a migration technique called "ballooning," where baby spiders climb to the top of tall vegetation and release silk balloons to be carried by the wind. It's believed that spiders can travel up to almost two miles in this manner, which explains why spiders are found on every continent—even Antarctica! Martyn noted that in some years the mass migration of spiders has caused entire fields to be covered in "angel hair." Martyn said angel hair could also arise after heavy rains or floods, where spiders tend to throw "silk" lines to pull themselves out of the water.

BEAR BREAKS INTO HOME AND PLAYS THE PIANO

According to security camera footage, a black bear broke into a Vail, Colorado home and played some very ordinary music on a piano before heading off to ransack the kitchen.

Homeowner Katie Hawley says she accidentally left a kitchen window unlocked, which must have been apparent to the bear, who simply slid it open to enter the home. When Katie returned the next morning, she found the damage caused by the "intruder," who had also consumed pancake syrup and a bag of chocolate bark. After reporting the incident, Katie reviewed the security footage, which showed the bear jumping onto its hind legs to play a single "unbearable" chord on her piano. Perhaps recognizing the need to practice, the bear returned several times after the incident, but Katie did not answer the knocks on the window.

MAN CALLS 911 TO COMPLAIN ABOUT HIS AGGRESSIVE CAT

Connecticut police say a man called 911 to report that his eight-pound cat bit him and was being so aggressive that he and his wife couldn't get back in their home!

It's reported that when the couple tried to get back in the house, the cat was waiting behind the door "in an aggressive manner" so they simply waited in the car. In a recording of the 911 call, which was made from the man's car in a parking lot, the man can be heard saying "I cannot go inside my home . . . my cat . . . attacked and scratched me in my leg and bit me." Police told the couple to stay away from the cat for the rest of the night.

Dumpster diving bear

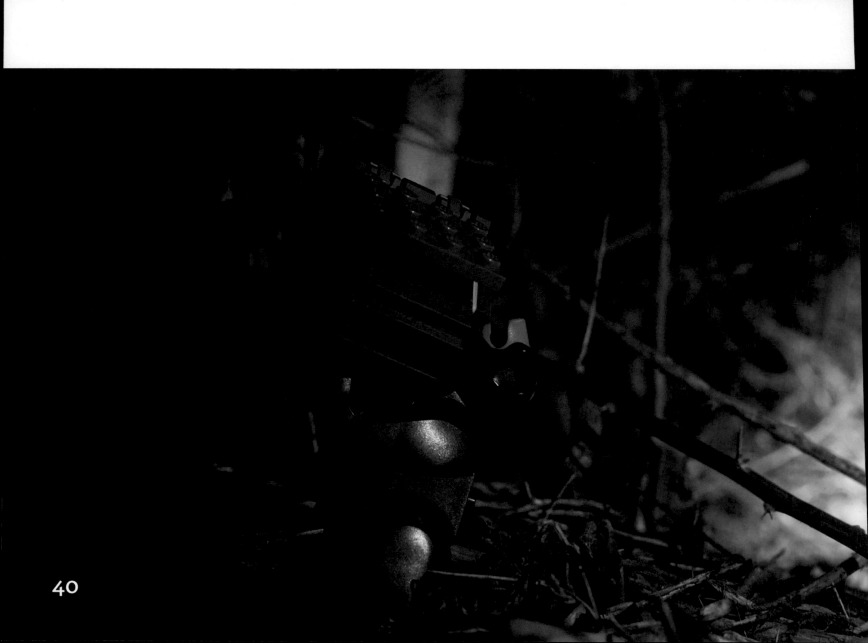

According to security footage from the Edelweiss restaurant in Colorado Springs, a hungry bear stole their entire dumpster for a late-night snack.

The sneaky feast was discovered when employees from the German restaurant arrived for work in the morning to find an entire dumpster tipped over in the parking lot. A review of security camera footage showed the smarter-than-your-average-bear dragging the dumpster fifty feet into the parking lot so that it could better access its tasty treats.

The restaurant posted the footage on its Facebook page with the caption "WOW. This must be the Mama," and believes the bear might be responsible for other dumpster dives.

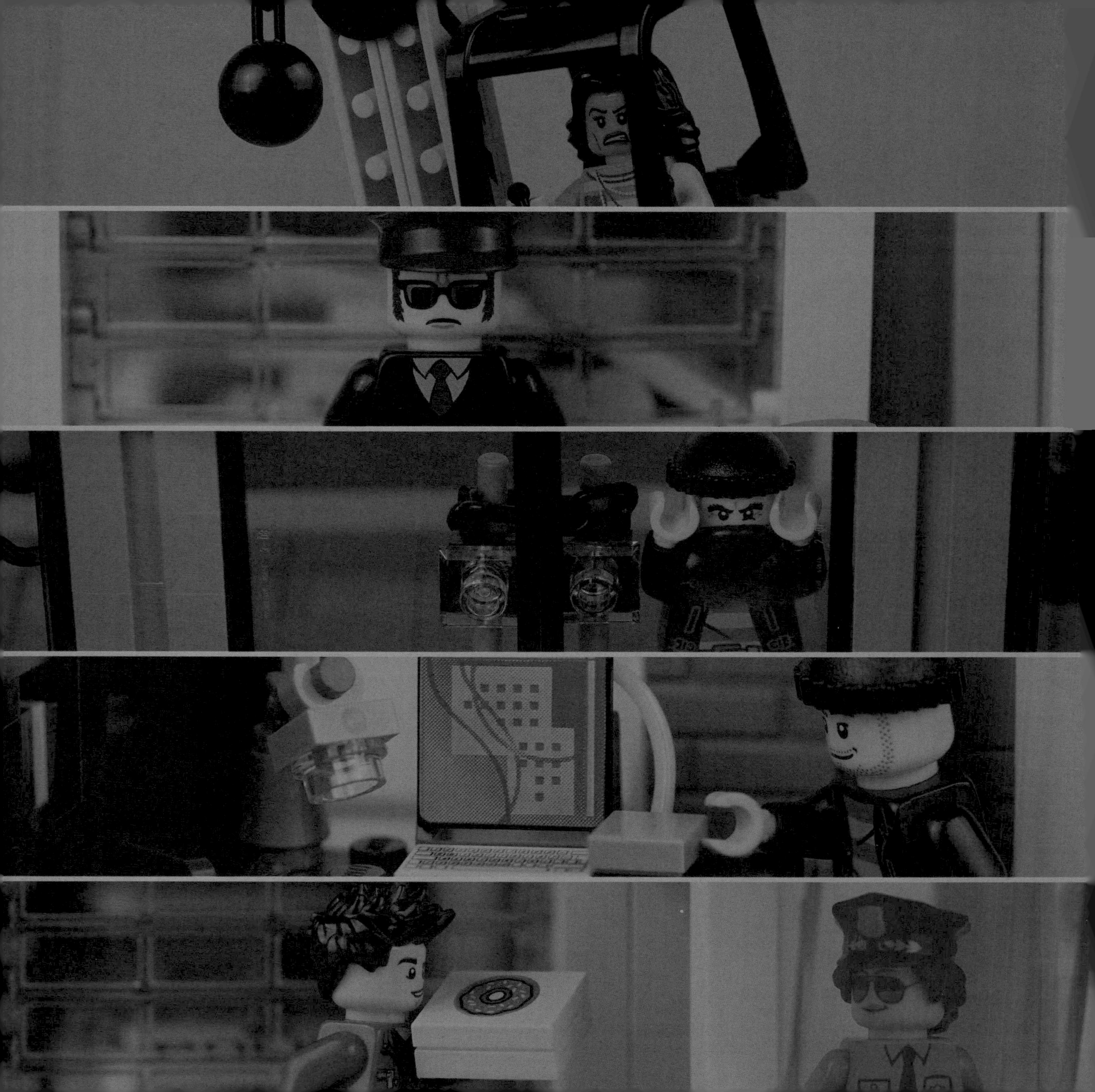

CHAPTER 3
CRIME DOESN'T PAY

THIEF RETURNS STOLEN LAPTOP'S CONTENTS TO ITS OWNER

A professor at Umeå University in Sweden lost ten years of work when his laptop was stolen, but a week after the theft, he received a USB stick with the contents of his laptop!

According to the professor, he left his laptop behind a stairwell in his apartment while he collected items from the building's laundry room. When he returned, the bag remained but not the laptop. The professor says he was devastated as he had been bad at backing up his computer, which was his life and contained a record of everything that had happened in the last ten years. The thief's actions made the professor "feel hope for humanity."

RESTAURANT THIEF COOKS, CLEANS UP, AND LEAVES TIP!

A man broke into a Long Island, New York restaurant, cooked himself a meal, cleaned up, and even left a tip!

According to surveillance footage from Nelly's Taqueria in Hicksville, the man took $100 from the cash register, then cooked himself rice, frijoles, shrimp, and chicken. Restaurant manager "Mike" observed that the man knew food safety rules, as he changed his gloves regularly, and "sifted the pot like a pro." After the feast, the thief scrubbed the dishes and collected crumbs from the floor! The thief must have been pleased, as he left $1 in the tip jar (presumably from the money he took). Mike said he'd hire the man if he wasn't breaking the law, but the footage was still forwarded to police for justice to be served (probably cold).

FLORIDA WOMAN HIRES BULLDOZER TO DEMOLISH NEIGHBOR'S HOME

A woman in St Augustine, Florida hired a bulldozer to demolish the home of a neighbor she did not like.

To carry out the outrageous plan, Ana Maria Moreta Folch obtained a key to her neighbor's home, convinced the heavy equipment company that she owned the neighbor's property, then asked for the mobile home to be razed. The owner called police when she returned home to find a pile of rubble. Folch was later arrested and charged with criminal mischief. According to police, Folch admitted to the deed and felt she did the neighborhood a favor by getting rid of the home, as it was being rented out to sketchy people. Only in Florida . . .

EARLY BURGLAR CATCHES NOTHING

Police in Des Moines, Iowa say a man tried to rob two banks but was unsuccessful because he arrived too early and the doors were locked!

According to security camera footage, a man whose face was covered by a red bandanna tried to enter a Marine Credit Union branch at 8:15 a.m., but was unsuccessful because it did not open until 11 a.m. that day. Later that morning, a man "described almost exactly like the first" was unable to enter a nearby First National Bank branch at 8:45 a.m. (which opened at 9 a.m. that day) after he spotted a police officer inside the bank. Perhaps it pays to be a not-so-early-bird sometimes?

Arrests made in relation to fake Ferraris

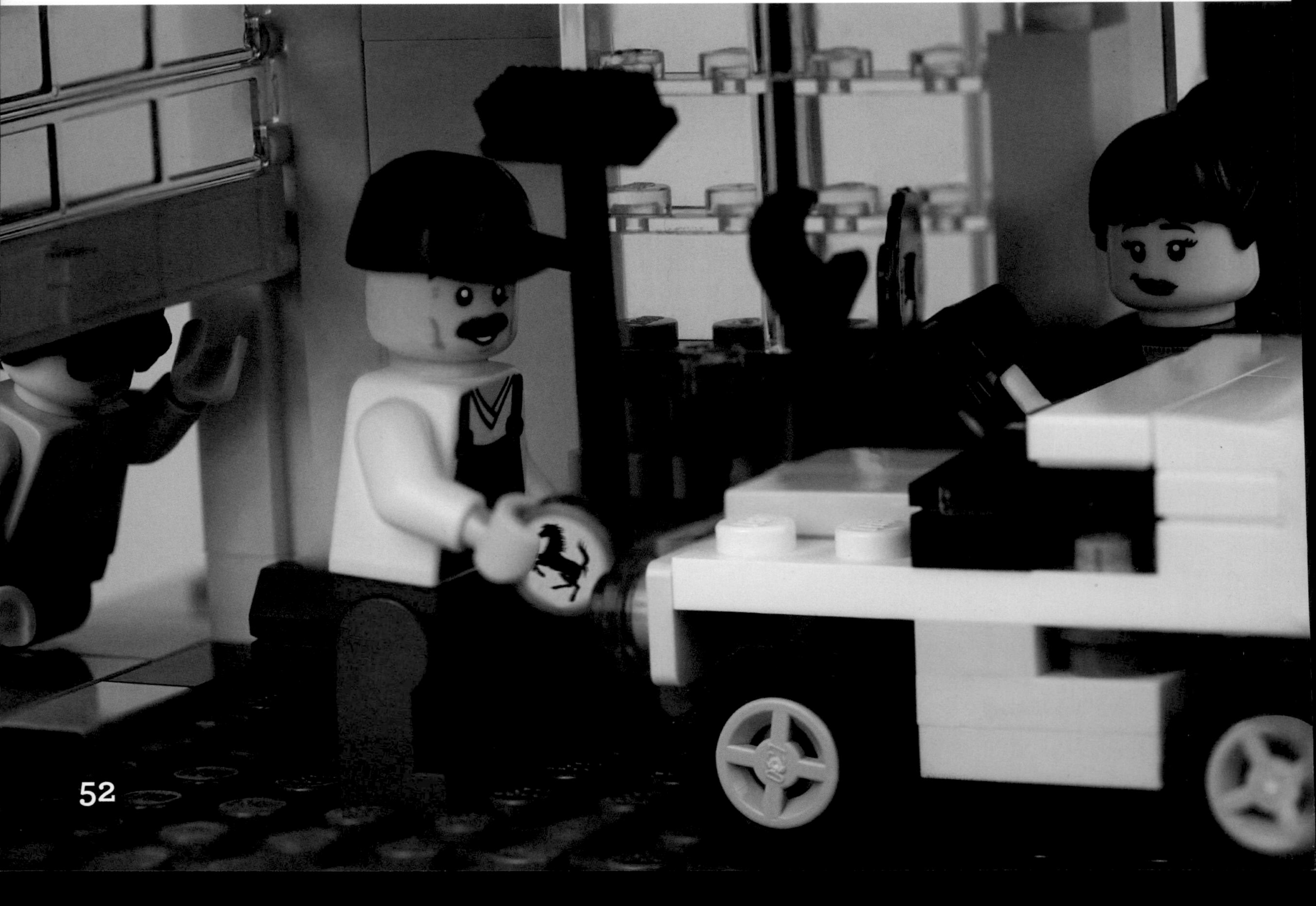

Three people were arrested for making and selling counterfeit Ferraris and Lamborghinis out of a workshop in Girona, Spain.

According to local media, the discovery of a fake Ferrari led police to the workshop and the network of second-hand websites used to sell the cars. During the raid, police reportedly found four completed Ferraris along with fourteen other cars in various states of transformation. It's believed that the luxury cars were created by fusing a Ferrari or Lamborghini body kit onto a Toyota chassis with fiberglass. Following this, emblems were then added, along with odometers and fake registration documents.

DODGY POSTMAN HOARDS MAIL

An Italian postman was arrested after 1,100 pounds of undelivered mail was found stashed in the garage of his home in Vicenza.

Workers from a recycling plant found the mail stored in plastic containers, with some of the mail dating back to 2010! The mail included leaflets from 2010 regional elections, tax forms, and utility bills. Police were then called to the home of the fifty-six-year-old man to make the arrest in what was described as the biggest ever seizure of undelivered mail in Italy. The "violation, misappropriation or destruction" of mail is a criminal offence in Italy, punishable by up to one year in prison.

The Vicenza postal service suspended the bad *postino*, then attempted to deliver the mail to the intended recipients.

FRIENDS UNWITTINGLY HELP MAN ROB A HOME

Police say a Great Falls, Montana man got his friends to unwittingly help him steal $40,000 worth of goods from another person's house by telling them he needed help moving!

One of Joseph Adams Jr.'s friends had even hired a U-Haul van, while another said he became suspicious when he saw military medals but was not aware of Joseph having served in the military. According to police, the real owner called 911 when he came home to find that he had been robbed. Joseph was charged with burglary and criminal mischief. Any takers to help move some art from a local gallery?

WANTED MAN BRINGS COPS A BOX OF DONUTS TO SETTLE BET

58

Wanted man Michael Zaydel handed himself into the Redford Police Department after he lost a bet as to whether their next Facebook post would get a thousand shares.

Zaydel (a.k.a. Champagne Torino), who was wanted on "existing warrants," told Redford Police in a private Facebook message that he would hand himself in with a box of donuts and clean up "every piece of litter around all your public schools" if their next post was shared 1,000 times. Redford Police accepted the challenge and asked the public to help them get the donuts and keep Redford clean at the same time. The post was shared more than 4,000 times and true to his word, Zaydel turned up with a box of donuts and a bagel!

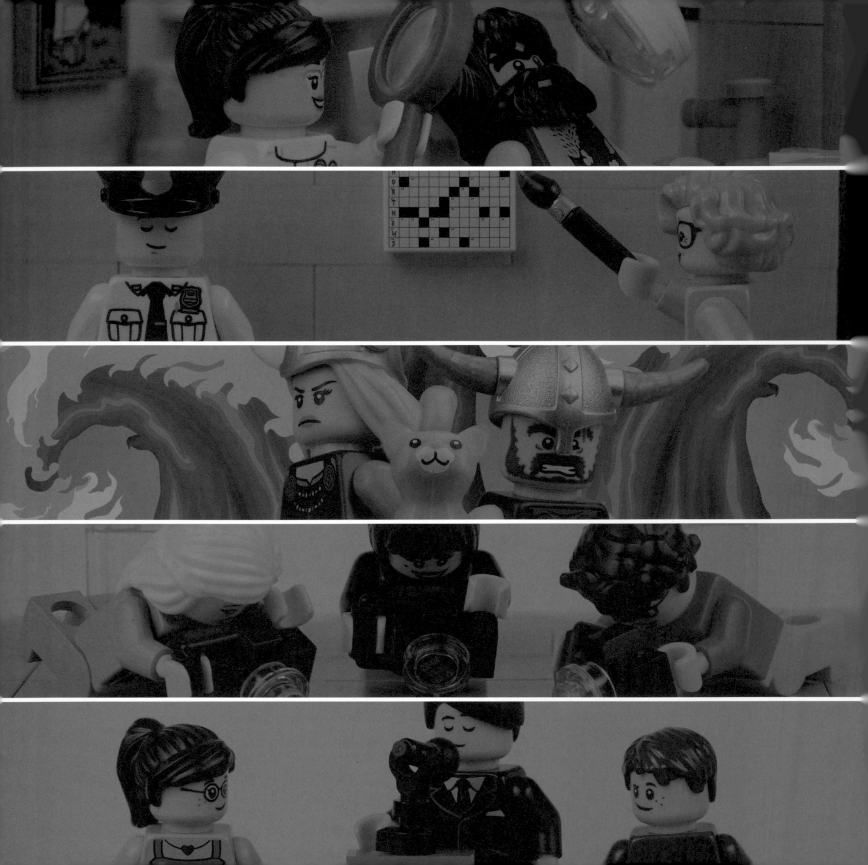

CHAPTER 4
ART, HISTORY, & CULTURE

A BANANA BY ANY OTHER NAME...

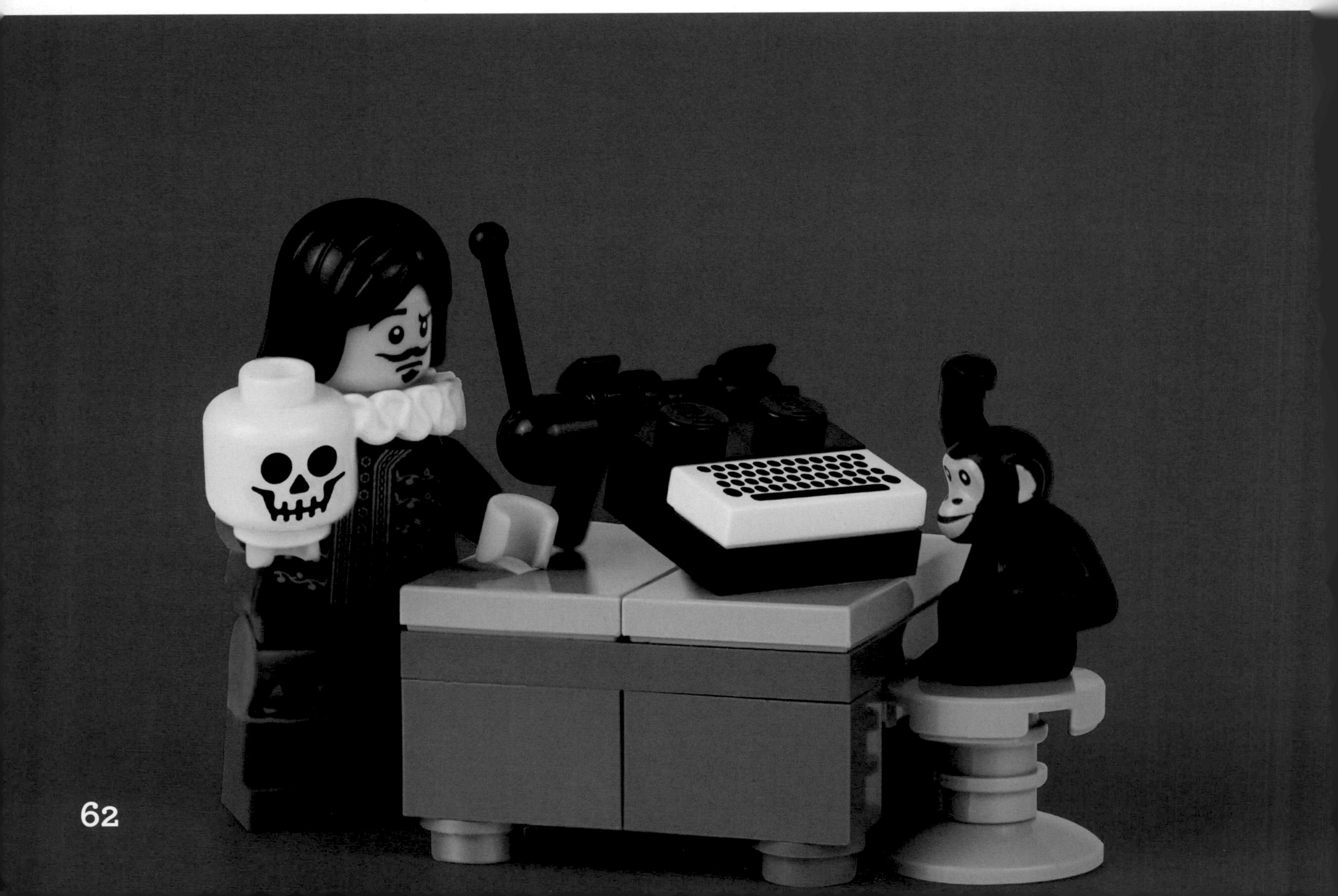

Thanks to scientists at Stanford University, monkeys are one step closer to recreating the complete works of Shakespeare!

During the study, monkeys were able to type "with their minds" after being fitted with a "multielectrode array." The system is designed to read brain signals and convert them into actions on the keyboard, which in this case meant that the monkeys tapped letters shown to them on a screen. The monkeys typed out *Hamlet* as well as passages from the *New York Times*, reaching speeds of 12 words per minute. Although similar technology already exists (such as eye or muscle tracking) the increased speed of Stanford's system could lead to improved communication options for the severely disabled.

Grandmother fills out crossword art piece

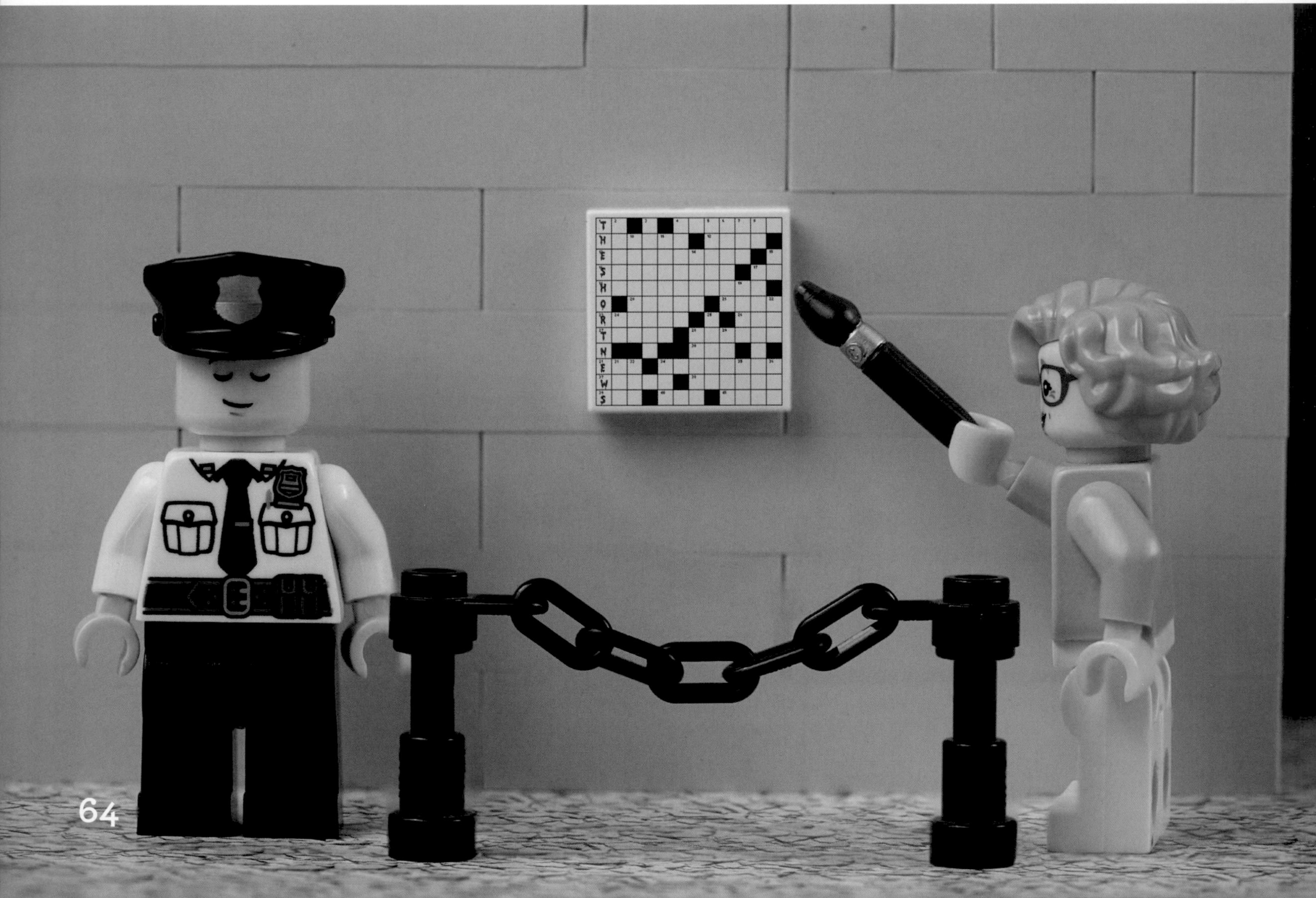

A crossword art piece was "filled in" by a ninety-one-year-old woman who thought the partially-completed crossword was an invitation to finish it!

The retired dentist was visiting the Nuremberg museum when she took it upon herself to fill in the squares of "Reading-Work Piece" by Arthur Köpcke. According to a local newspaper, the woman knew the English word for *Mauer* (wall), so she rushed to write it where indicated, using a pen of course. The grandmother told police that the phrase "Insert Words" (already written in the puzzle) was an invitation to complete the puzzle and that the museum should have made it clear this was not the case. The 1977 piece is insured for $100,000.

Epic spelling bee

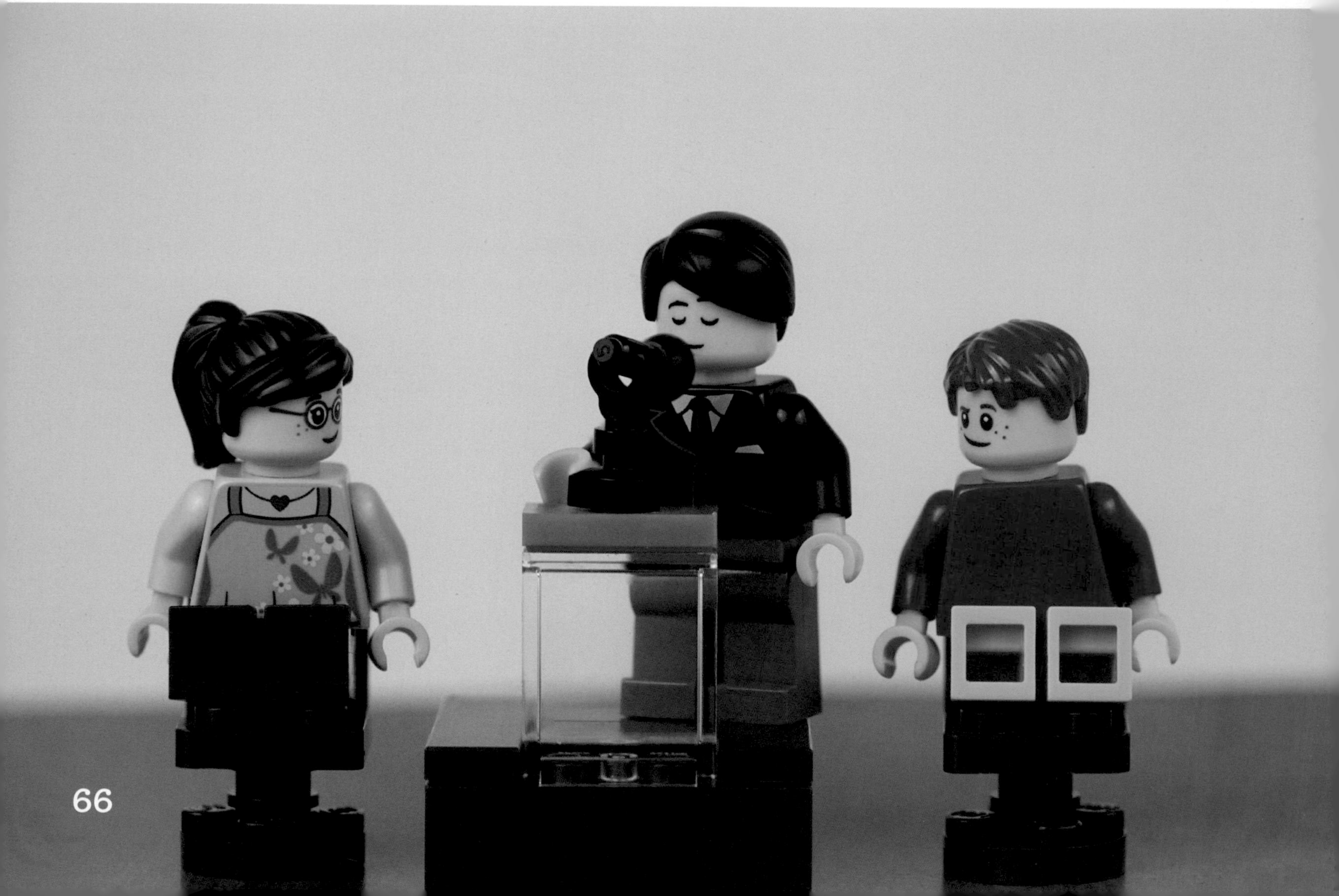

After 95 rounds and more than two weeks, a marathon spelling bee in Kansas City, Missouri between two students finally ended when the runner-up misspelled the word "stifling."

Fifth-grader Sophia Hoffman and seventh-grader Kush Sharma dueled for sixty-six rounds in the Jackson County Spelling Bee before organizers ran out of words provided by the Scripps National Spelling Bee. At a special spell-off in front of an overflow crowd, Sophia and Kush cruised through words such as "slobber" and "boodle" before Sophia stumbled with "stifling," which allowed Kush to take out the title with the word "definition." Following the competition, Sophia and Kush became close friends and went on to become celebrities in Kansas City.

AUDIENCE MEMBER TRIES TO USE FAKE POWER OUTLET AT BROADWAY SHOW

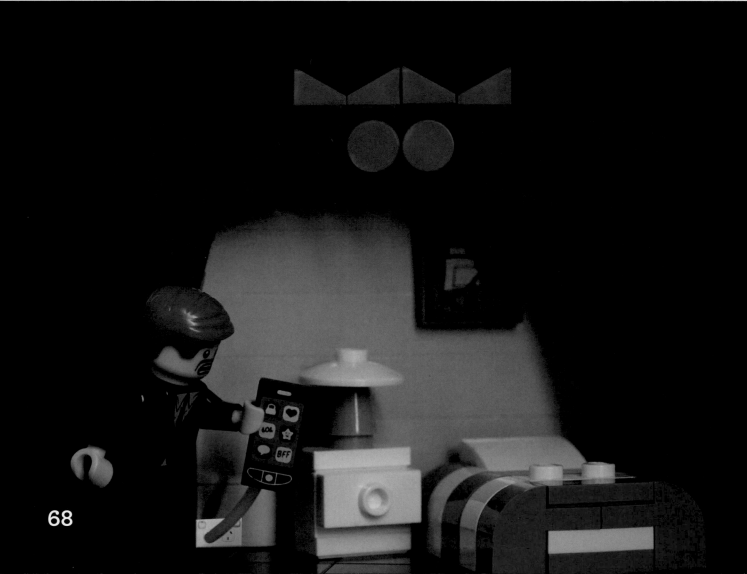

An audience member actually walked onto the stage of Broadway show *Hand to God* and tried to use a fake power outlet to charge his mobile phone!

The incident occurred at Booth Theatre about two minutes before the show was set to begin, startling the crew and theatergoers. Although the event was recounted by many, fellow audience member Chris York described the moment in a Facebook post, pointing out that there were no stairs to the stage so the man had to leap onto the stage and walk fifteen feet to reach the visibly fake power outlet. According to *Broadway Adjacent*, the man asked "Well, where can I charge it?" after he was ushered offstage!

EINSTEIN'S THEORY ON HAPPINESS SELLS FOR $1.56 MILLION!

In 1922, Albert Einstein gave a courier his theory on happiness, written on hotel stationery, which was sold at Jerusalem auction house nearly one hundred years later for $1.56 million!

While staying at the Imperial Hotel Tokyo, the Nobel Prize-winning physicist did not have money to tip the courier, so he gave him two notes and said "Maybe if you're lucky those notes will become much more valuable than just a regular tip". The first note, which sold for $1.56 million, read: "A calm and humble life will bring more happiness than the pursuit of success and the constant restlessness that comes with it." The second note, which sold for $240,000, read: "Where there's a will, there's a way." Funnily enough, the seller was the nephew of the courier!

JUDGE RULES THAT "HAPPY BIRTHDAY" IS OWNED BY THE PEOPLE

A US Federal Judge ruled that nobody owns the "Happy Birthday" song, declaring the copyright held by Warner/Chappell Music to be invalid.

US District Judge George King said that Kentucky sisters Patty and Mildred Hill did not try to obtain copyright protection when they wrote the song in 1889 under the original title "Good Morning To All." Furthermore, the song was already in the public domain when the first copyright over the song was claimed in 1935. As a result, Judge King ruled that Warner/Chappell Music did not own the lyrics to the song and had no right to charge for the song's use. Warner/Chappell Music later agreed to pay back $14 million to those who have paid licensing fees to use the song.

CATS TRAVELED WITH VIKINGS!

DNA sequenced from 290 cats from thirty archaeological sites in the Middle East, Africa, and Europe indicates that cats traveled with Vikings!

According to the study performed by Eva-Maria Geigl and colleagues from L'Institut Jacques Monod in Paris, cats spread across the world in two waves. First at the birth of agriculture in eastern Mediterranean, and second when they moved from Egypt to Asia and Africa, most likely through seafaring people such as Vikings. In both cases, cats were most likely kept around because of their ability to keep rodent numbers down. Some proof? A cat with Egyptian mitochondrial DNA was found on a Viking site in northern Germany dating between 700 and 1000 AD!

BOY DISCOVERS MILLION-YEAR-OLD FOSSIL BY TRIPPING OVER IT!

A ten-year-old boy discovered the million-year-old fossil of a prehistoric creature when he fell on it while hiking with his parents in Las Cruces, New Mexico.

Jude Sparks says he was running when he tripped on part of a tusk belonging to the Stegomastodon, which is from the Pleistocene era and believed to be an ancestor to the modern-day elephant. The creature is not a dinosaur, as T-Rex and friends lived during the Mesozoic era which ended 66 million years ago. As the fossil was located on private land, it took several months to commence excavations. Chemical hardeners were applied to keep the "deceptively delicate" bones intact, with the fossil then coated in plaster for transport to its current home, the New Mexico State University's Vertebrate Museum.

Glasses left on art gallery floor as a prank

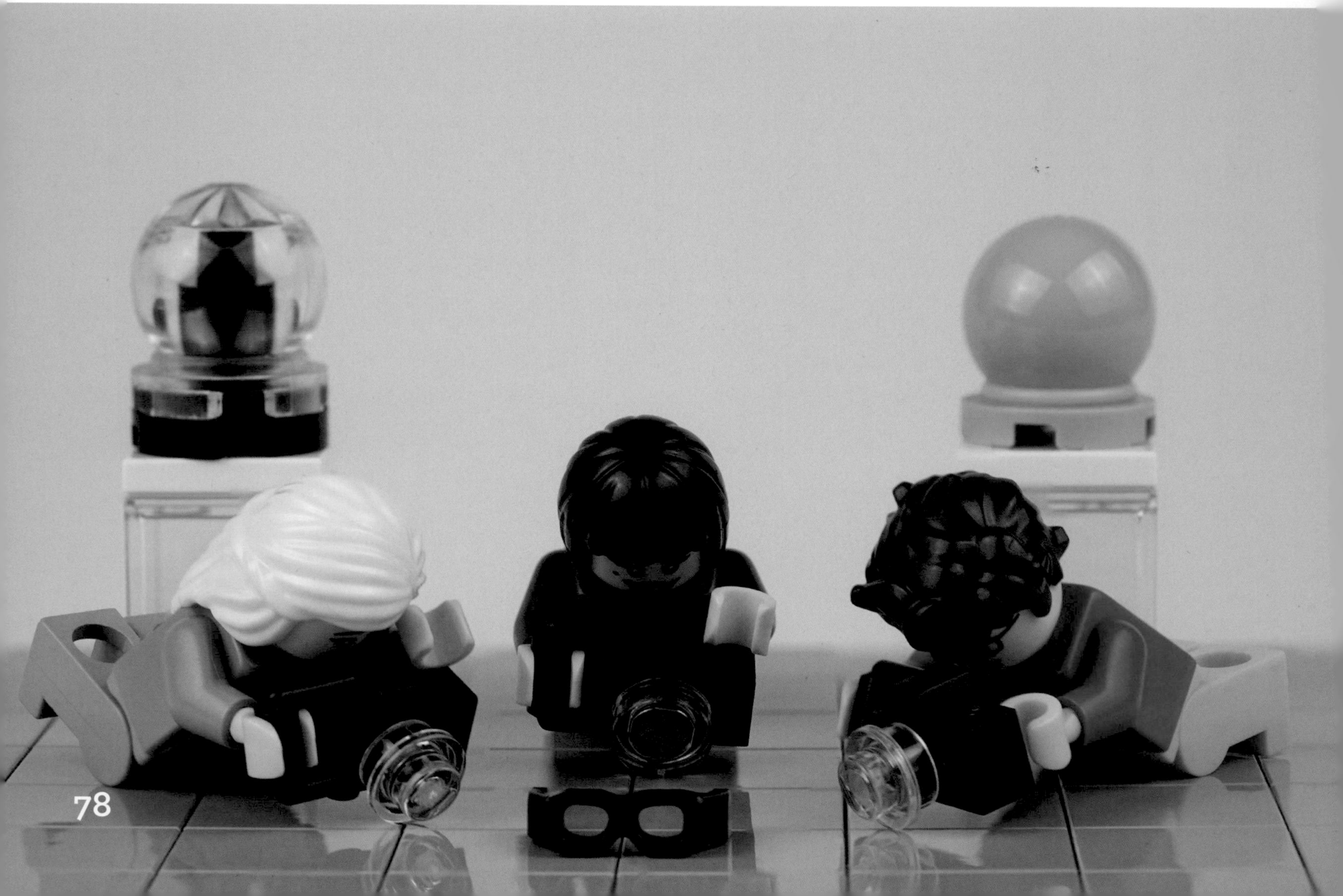

When pranksters left a pair of glasses on the floor of an art gallery, it didn't take long for people to crowd around the intriguing "installation."

US teenagers Kevin Nguyen and TJ Khayatan questioned the merit of some pieces at the San Francisco Museum of Modern Art, so they left a pair of black glasses below an official-looking piece of paper to see what would happen. Sure enough, people took notice and started to crowd around the exhibit. Almost certainly laughing, Kevin and TJ admired their handy work from a distance and took photos of the people taking photos of the glasses, which they later posted to Twitter. The photographs went viral, but they also generated genuine discussion about how we interpret art.

Neanderthal teeth reveal they ate plants and used aspirin!

Neanderthals did not focus on dental hygiene, which is great news for scientists who used their hardened dental plaque (also known as dental calculus) to better understand how they lived.

Bacteria and DNA extracted from sets of teeth belonging to three Neanderthals from Belgium and Spain revealed that the Belgian Neanderthals ate mostly meat (such as woolly rhino and wild sheep), whereas the Spanish Neanderthal's diet included mostly vegetables (such as moss and mushrooms). Interestingly, one of the samples indicated that poplar bark may have eaten to treat illness, as it contains Penicillium and an active ingredient in aspirin. It's believed that the tested samples were 48,000 years old, making it the oldest dental plaque to ever be genetically analyzed.

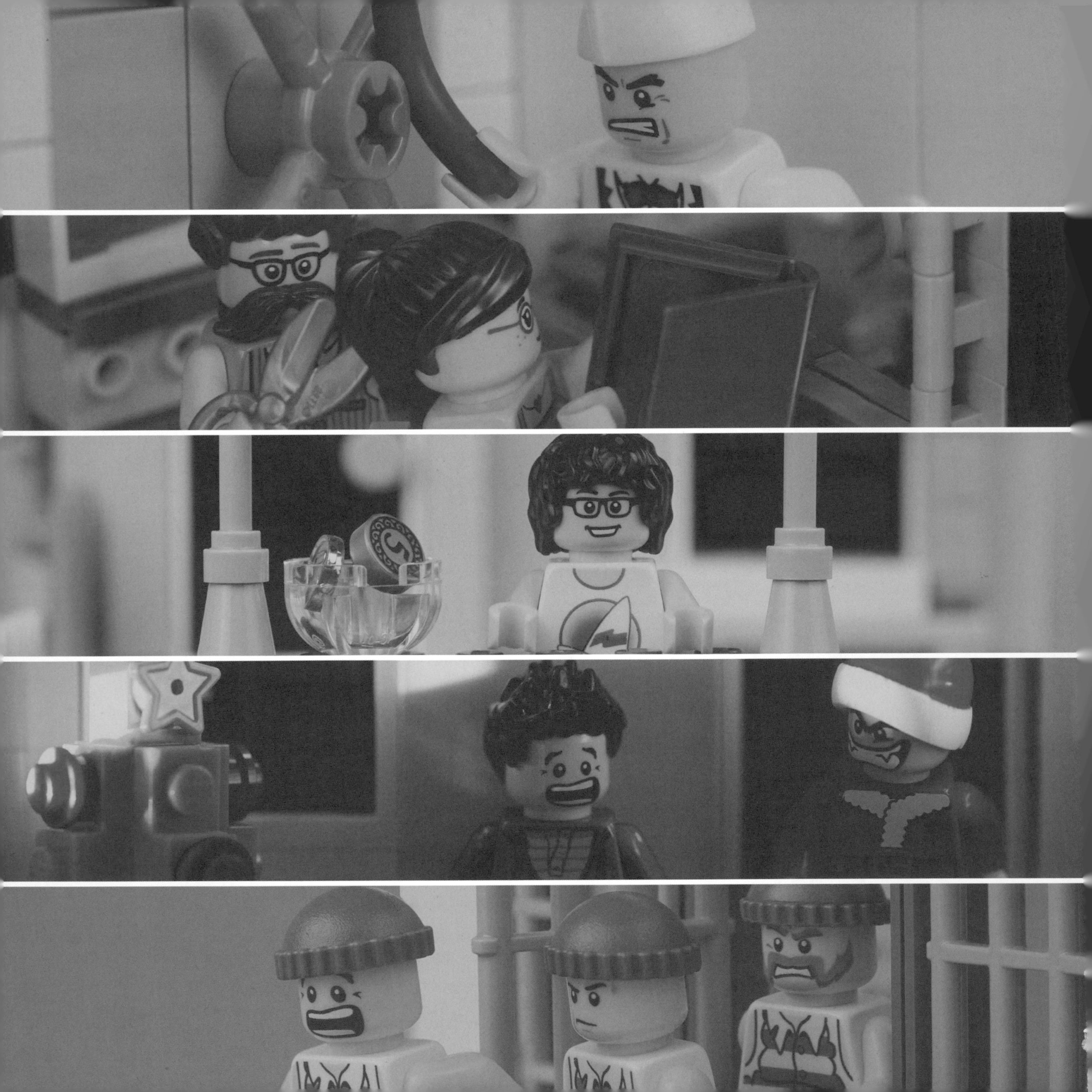

CHAPTER 5
HEROES & QUICK THINKERS

BARBER GIVES FREE HAIRCUTS TO KIDS WHO READ ALOUD IN HIS CHAIR

A barber in Dubuque, Iowa offered free haircuts to children who read a book aloud in his chair.

Courtney Holmes told kids to choose a book from his table and offered to help those who couldn't read the book. Although the project started as a "Back to School Bash," Holmes says he made it a monthly event to promote early literacy and continue improving children's reading skills. Many people have already started donating books to the cause! Holmes' project took place at Spark Family Hair Salon, which led to a partnership with the My Brother's Keeper program and the Foundation of Greater Dubuque to further promote early literacy.

Boy calls 911 to warn them about the Grinch

A five-year-old boy in Mississippi became scared after watching "How the Grinch Stole Christmas," so he called 911 to warn police about the Grinch's plans!

TyLon Pittman told the 911 dispatcher: "I just want to tell you something. Watch for that little Grinch. Because the Grinch is gonna steal Christmas, okay?" Shortly after, police attended the home to reassure TyLon that they would protect him from the Grinch and that Christmas would be safe. Police later invited TyLon to the station and told him he could lock up the Grinch, who was waiting in a police car. TyLon placed the Grinch in a holding cell, but in true Christmas spirit he let him out. TyLon says he'd like to be a police officer one day.

INMATES BREAK OUT OF JAIL TO HELP UNCONSCIOUS GUARD

A group of Texas inmates broke out of a holding cell to save a prison guard who had lost consciousness!

The inmates were in the Weatherford District Courts Building awaiting court appearances when the guard slumped to the floor. When their screams were not heard, the group of eight men burst out of the holding cell, found the guard had no pulse, then tried to use his radio to call for help. Deputies heard the noise downstairs and came to assist, with emergency crew following soon after. Even though the guard had keys and a gun, one of the inmates, Nick Kelton, said this never crossed his mind, adding that "if he falls down, I'll help him." The guard was said to be recovering from an apparent heart attack.

Teen crowdfunded his tuition in 1987

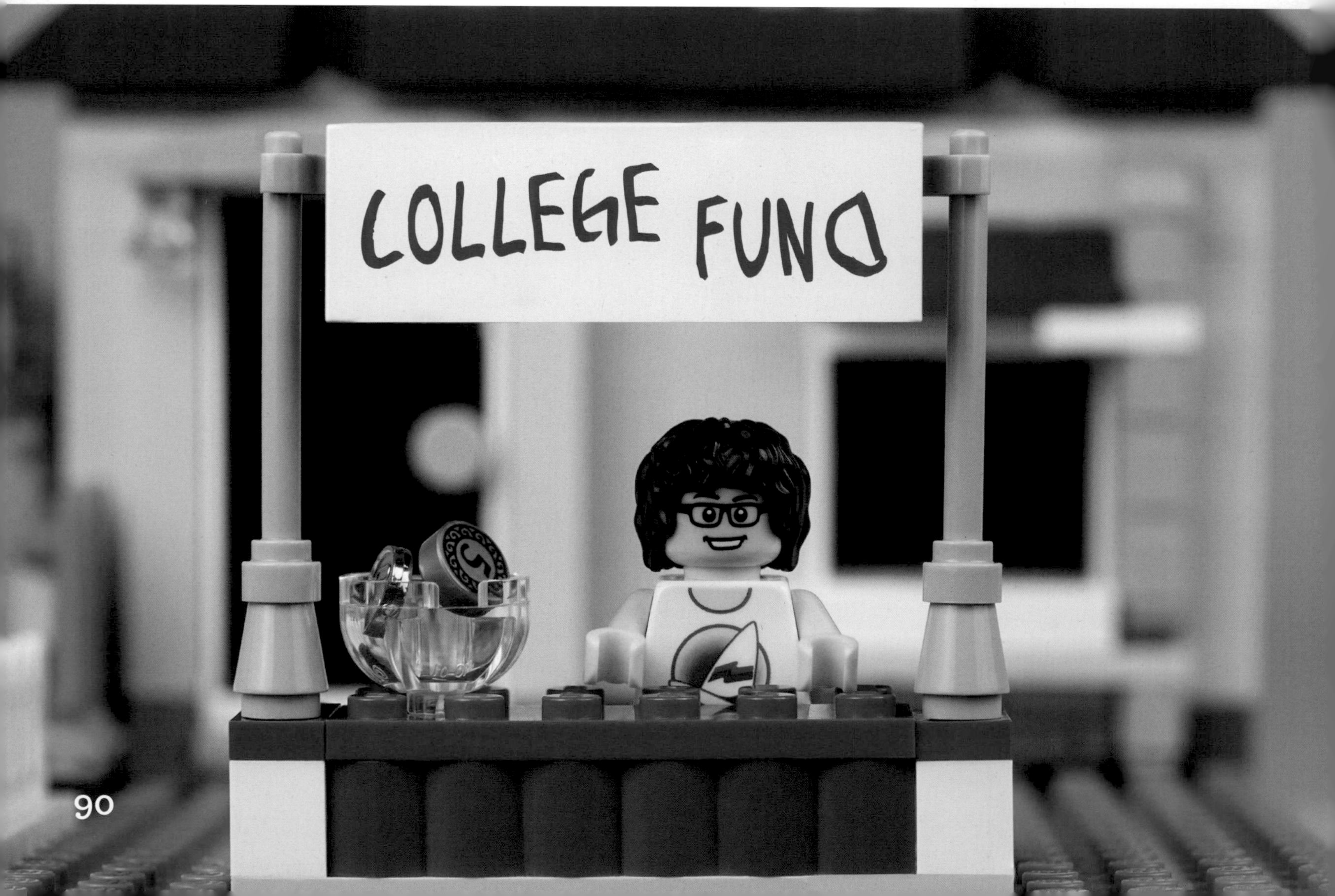
COLLEGE FUND

Before the internet went live to the world, and much before crowdfunding became a norm, eighteen-year-old Mike Hayes crowdfunded his $28,000 University of Illinois tuition costs by asking 2.8 million Americans to donate a penny to his college fund.

According to Hayes, this was probably "the only idea" he ever had, but he needed the help of *Chicago Tribune* columnist Bob Greene, who shared Hayes's story and told readers to "put that penny in the envelope." Despite postage costs, readers sent a total of approximately 2.9 million pennies. At one point, Hayes received more than twenty-six feet of mail in one day!

In 1991, the "Penny Man" graduated debt-free with a degree in food science and planned to donate the surplus $1,000 to one of the families that sent him money.

AUSSIE HERO SAVED THE DAY IN HIS JOCKS

In one of the most Aussie stories ever, a Brisbane man recounted how he woke up at 2 a.m. when a car crashed into a shop next door, then, dressed in only his underwear, confronted the driver! Daniel McConnell told the absconding driver: "What are you doing mate . . . like, you can't be leaving the scene." The driver told Daniel not to be a hero and drove off, but didn't count on Daniel chasing him in his own car (still in his underwear), then helping the police to find the man. Daniel added: "All I had was me jocks on and I was chasing him up the street. And I was like, mate!" In true Aussie spirit, Daniel said he did it because it's important to look after your mates.

BUTCHER USES GIANT SAUSAGE TO ESCAPE FROM A FREEZER

A butcher in Totnes, Devon used a giant 3.3 lb blood sausage to bash his way out of a walk-in freezer when a gust of wind caused the door to slam shut.

According to seventy-year-old butcher Chris McCabe, nobody could hear him banging on the door, so he knew he'd have to kick his way out of the freezer, which stores meat at -20°C (-4°F). Unfortunately, the safety button was frozen solid, so Chris searched for a tool. Chris says he could have used a roll of beef, but chose the 1.5-ft. sausage instead because it had a nice flat end "like one of those police battering rams," which he used to escape. Although Chris knows the black pudding saved his life, he got the safety button repaired, just in case.

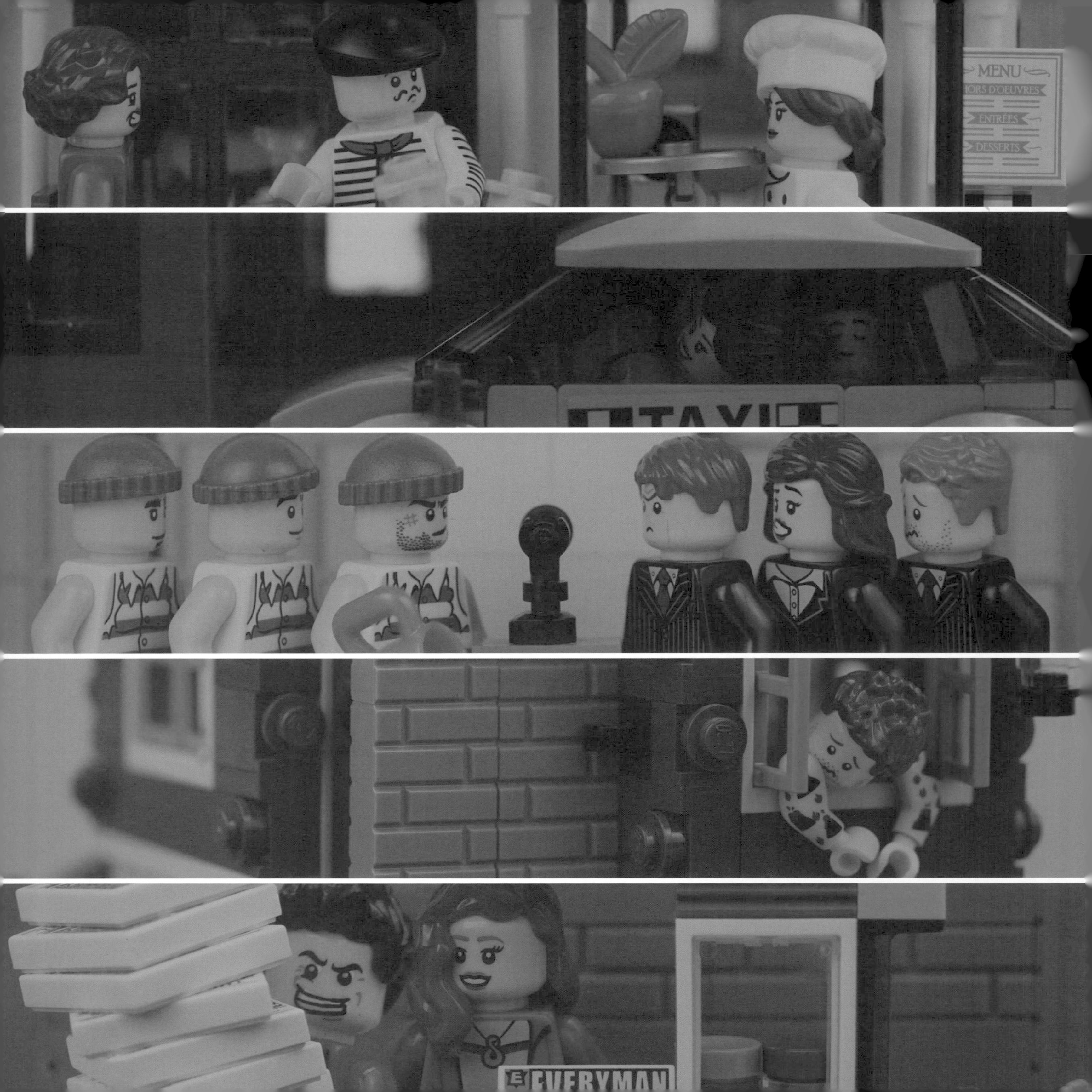
MENU
ENTRÉES
DESSERTS
TAXI
EVERYMAN

CHAPTER 6
STRANGER THAN FICTION

DUTCH SOLDIERS FORCED TO SHOUT BANG DURING SHOOTING DRILLS

An ammunition shortage reportedly forced Dutch soldiers to imitate the sound of firing their weapons in shooting drills by shouting "Bang! Bang!"

According to a Defense Ministry email seen by Dutch broadcaster RTL, the Dutch army has long suffered from a shortage of ammunition, but the situation became dire when soldiers were instructed to train with their weapons even if they had no bullets. It was reported that the Dutch Government increased its defense budget in 2015, with ammunition stockpiles to be replenished once funding became available.

PRANKSTERS BUILT BRICK WALL IN FRONT OF MAN'S DOOR

A German man came home from a night shift to find that somebody had built a brick wall in front of his front door!

It's reported that the incident occurred in Mainhausen, Hesse, and that the man was forced to borrow an axe to demolish the wall. According to a police spokesperson, a few people may have been involved in the suspected prank, but he added that "it's a crime and no joke." Although police had no idea who did this, they were of the view that it was the sort of thing that somebody will eventually boast about at a bar. Some reports indicated that the man was asleep when the wall was built, which explains the variation in this picture.

NY PRISON INMATES DEFEAT HARVARD DEBATING TEAM

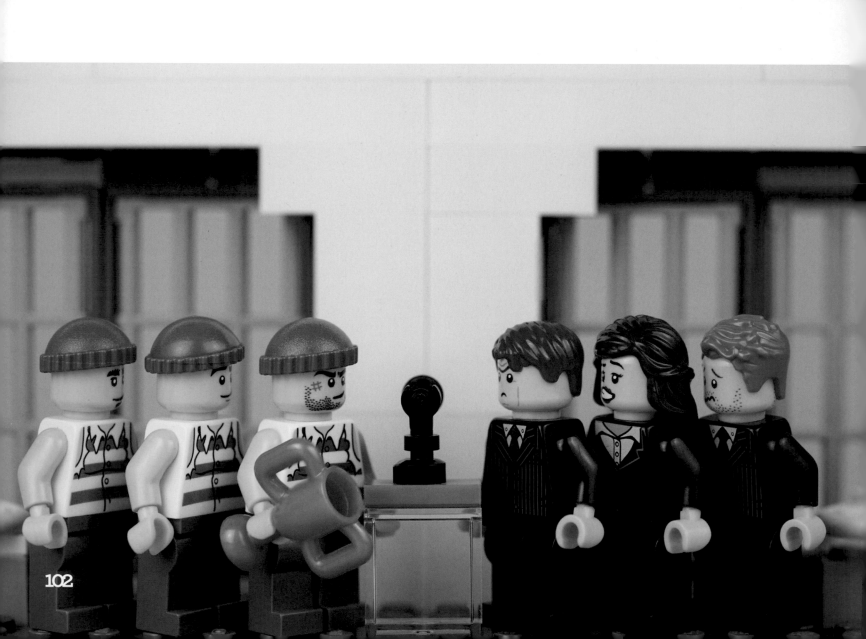

A group of New York prison inmates defeated the Harvard Debate Team, who were the national debate champions!

The debate took place at the maximum security Eastern New York Correctional Facility. A panel of neutral judges awarded the debate to the inmates, who were tasked with arguing that public schools should be able to turn away the children of people who entered the US illegally. In a post on its Facebook account, Harvard called the inmates phenomenally intelligent and said there are few teams they are prouder of having lost a debate to. Fifteen percent of inmates at the Facility take courses at the nearby Bard College, with many continuing studies at Columbia and Yale. The debate club was established to help inmates articulate their learnings.

RUSSIAN BOYS TUNNEL OUT OF KINDERGARTEN TO BUY A JAGUAR!

Two Russian five-year-old boys used toy spades to dig their way out of a kindergarten, walked 2 km to a luxury car dealership, then tried to buy a Jaguar!

According to Russia's *Komsomolskaya Pravda*, the duo had started digging a hole under a property fence a few days before they made their escape during a supervised walk in the kindergarten grounds. After trekking to the luxury car showroom, the boys are said to have told a woman that they wanted to buy a "grown up car," but didn't have any money. The woman then drove the boys to a police station. It's reported that although the boys' parents did not lodge a complaint against the kindergarten, the relevant supervisor was fired.

GRANDMOTHER SURVIVES 4 DAYS IN BATHROOM BY KNITTING AND EATING MINTS

A British grandmother trapped in a public restroom for four days used the hand dryer to keep warm, ate mints to keep her spirits up and knitted to keep herself occupied.

Gladys Phillips says she didn't realize the bathroom was not yet open to the public, with the door locking behind her as she walked in. Nobody realized Gladys was missing as she lives on her own and doesn't have a phone. Gladys "sat on the loo," knitted a scarf using her new ball of pink wool, and chewed on Mint Imperials she'd just purchased with her pension until she was rescued by a builder. According to the *Suffolk Gazette*, this incident highlights the hospitable design of the new restrooms.

MAN TRIES TO BUY EVERY SINGLE NEWSPAPER TO HIDE SECRET

A man bought nearly 1,000 copies of a New York newspaper in an effort to prevent people from reading about his drunk-driving arrest!

It's reported that the man was arrested for drunk driving in Wayne County, and that he later refused to be fingerprinted, and didn't want to be photographed or have his mugshot in the newspaper. However, the newspaper obtained a mugshot from the county jail and printed it along with the story. According to the newspaper's owner and editor, the man bought nearly 1,000 copies at $1.25 each. Unfortunately for the man, even though he bought so many copies, *the Times of Wayne County* is a 12,000-circulation newspaper with an online presence . . .

No butter means no croissants...

A major butter shortage in France led to supply issues in supermarkets, with opportunists taking advantage of the high demand by selling butter on the internet at ridiculous prices.

From April 2016 to October 2017, the value of butter rose from $3,000 per ton to $8,600 per ton. It's believed that the shortage was caused by low milk production and an increase in demand for French butter (and in general, butter over margarine). According to French baking lobby group the Federation des Entrepreneurs de la Boulangerie, this was a "major crisis" for France's annual 8.5 billion Euro baking industry.

ITALIAN MARATHON RUNNER WINS AFTER OTHER COMPETITORS TAKE WRONG TURN

Italian marathon runner Eyob Ghebrehiwet Faniel won the Venice Marathon after the race favorites took a wrong turn!

Approximately 25 km (16 miles) into the race, some of the favorites Gilbert Kipleting Chumba, David Kiprono Metto, Kipkemei Mutai, and Abdulahl Dawud were among a leading group of six runners when the motorcycle "guide" left the marathon route (as was planned at this stage), taking the group 100 meters off course. The error cost the group about two minutes, which allowed Faniel, who was originally one minute behind the leading pack, to claim the title with a time of two hours, twelve minutes and sixteen seconds. Faniel is the first Italian to win the Venice Marathon in twenty-two years.

FRENCH SCRABBLE WINNER DOESN'T EVEN SPEAK FRENCH!

A New Zealand man who doesn't speak French managed to win a French-language Scrabble competition by memorizing a French dictionary!

Nigel Richards from Christchurch is a Scrabble legend, having previously taken out the English world Scrabble titles in 2007 and 2011. To claim the French title, Nigel defeated Schelick Ilagou Rekawe from French-speaking Gabon in West Africa. Organizers say that Nigel memorized a French Scrabble dictionary in nine weeks and the French Scrabble Federation tweeted that Nigel's win was "amazing." According to professional Scrabble players, when played at a competitive level, the game is more about memorizing (rather than understanding) words, which might explain Nigel's win. Still, Nigel is an incredibly deserving and talented *gagnant* (winner).

London cab driver turns his taxi into a hotel room

During the London Olympics, a taxi driver turned his cab into a hotel for one, complete with a bed (covered with a Union Jack blanket), curtains, solar-powered fridge, and a Paddington Bear Teddy.

David Weekes advertised the a $60 a night "hotel" on an online rental website, with the main condition that guests accommodate his schedule. Notably, David needed guests to "check out" in the morning so that he could start his driving shift. According to Weekes, guests could park the taxi outside his home and use his bathroom facilities, or park elsewhere permissible by law. Weekes decided to rent out his taxi to make up for a predicted fall in revenue during the Olympics due to taxi drivers' exclusion from special Olympic lanes.

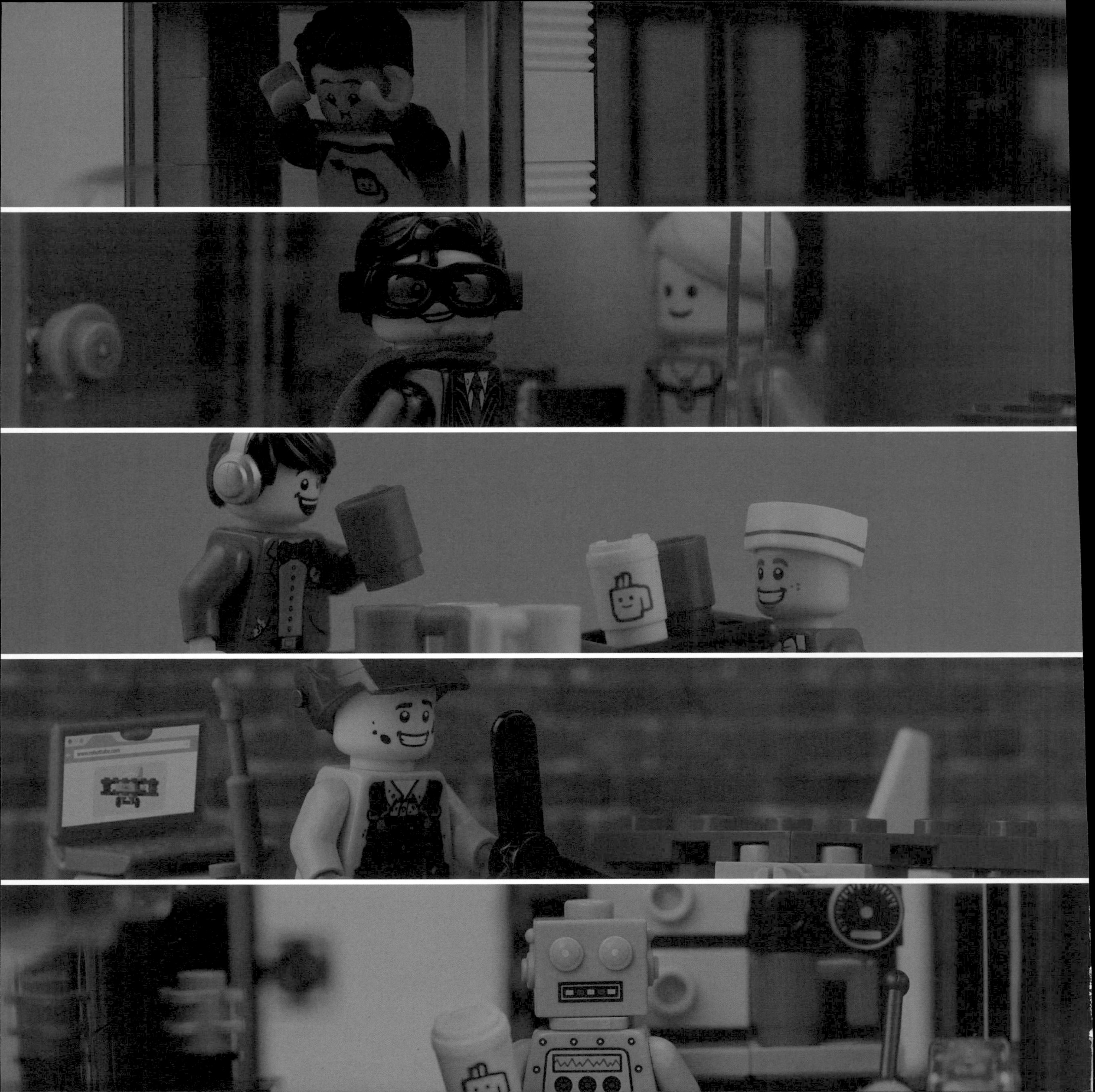

CHAPTER 7
SCIENCE & TECHNOLOGY

Cambodian man built his own plane by watching YouTube videos

A Cambodian man who had never been on a plane built his own plane using recycled materials and watching YouTube videos!

Paen Long, a thirty-year-old car mechanic with a longstanding passion for aviation, took three years and $10,000 to complete the one-seater aircraft, which he based on a Japanese plane used in WWII. The plane was made from an old gas container, with a car dashboard control panel and a plastic chair with sawn-off legs for the pilot's seat. Paen says he was emotional during his first launch in March 2017 because he couldn't bear the things his neighbors were saying when he reached a height of fifty meters before crashing to the ground. Paen blames the failure on the weight of the aircraft (500 kg) and is now trying to build a seaplane.

COFFEE MIGHT HELP YOU LIVE LONGER

According to the largest study of its kind, drinking coffee can significantly reduce the chance of dying from causes including heart disease, cancer, stroke, diabetes, and kidney disease!

The sixteen-year study was conducted among 520,000 people in ten European countries and 185,000 African-Americans, Japanese-Americans, and Latinos. The results? Those who drank one cup of coffee (approximately 250 ml) had a twelve percent lower risk of death, whereas people who drank three or more cups had an eighteen percent lower risk of lethal ailments! Thankfully, for those sensitive to caffeine, there appears to be no advantage between drinking decaf or caffeinated coffee, as the benefits are believed to exist in the antioxidant plant compounds in coffee.

Robot barista makes and serves coffee in Tokyo

A café has opened up in Shibuya, Japan where the coffee is made and served by the sole staff member—a robot!

Like other places in Japan, you pay for coffee at a vending machine, but this time you take your ticket (which has a QR code) to be scanned by the robot inside Henn na Café (Weird Café). A cup of coffee costs 320 yen (US $2.90), but the braggadocio is free, with the robot claiming that it "can brew coffee better than the human beings down the road." However, if you're in a rush, the robot reportedly takes four minutes to make and serve a cup of coffee, but at least it cleans up afterwards! According to the café's owner, the cafe only needs one staff member, aside from the engineer that maintains the robot.

SCIENCE SAYS THAT **NOT** MAKING YOUR BED IS HEALTHY

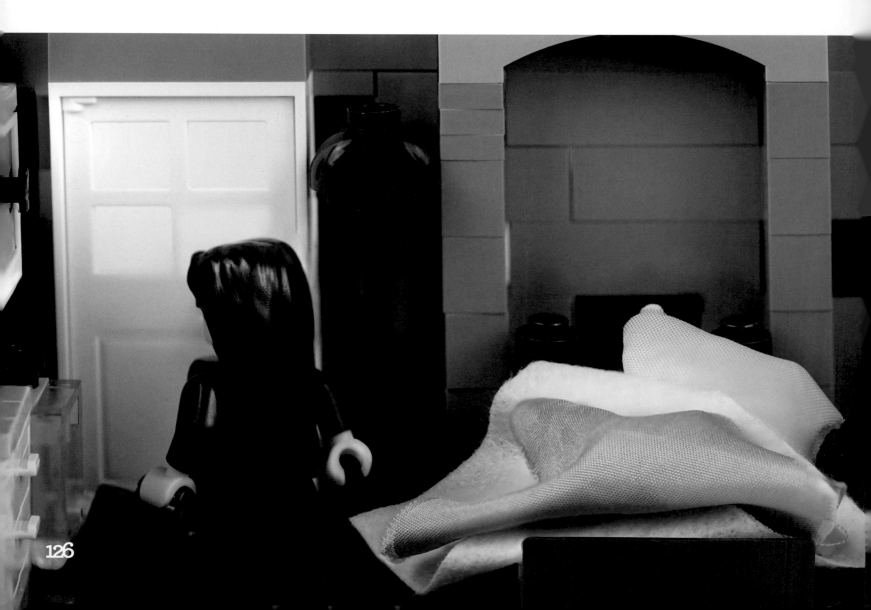

According to a study from Kingston University, NOT making your bed may be better for your health!

The average bed is home to up to 1.5 million house dust mites, which feed on flakes of human skin and are thought to be a major cause of asthma and other allergies. According to Dr. Stephen Pretlove at the university, mites survive by taking in water from the atmosphere using small glands on the outside of their body. However, by leaving the bed unmade, moisture is removed from the sheets causing mites to dehydrate and die. Hopefully science can release some studies on whether washing the dishes or taking out the trash are in fact good for your health!

CLARK KENT'S GLASSES WERE THE PERFECT DISGUISE

How did the city of Metropolis fail to recognize that Clark Kent was Superman? According to a study from the University of York, wearing glasses might be an adequate disguise, especially if you haven't seen that person before.

In the study, participants were shown three pairs of faces: (1) Both wore glasses. (2) Neither had glasses. (3) One had glasses and the other didn't. When asked to decide whether each pair showed the same person, accuracy was eighty percent in categories (1) and (2) but was six percent less when only one face had glasses. It's believed this is attributable to a cognitive disorder called prosopagnosia (face blindness) that impairs the ability to recognize familiar faces. While this wouldn't prevent Lois from recognizing Clark, it might affect a significant portion of the population making such an identification.

Britain introduces its first poo bus

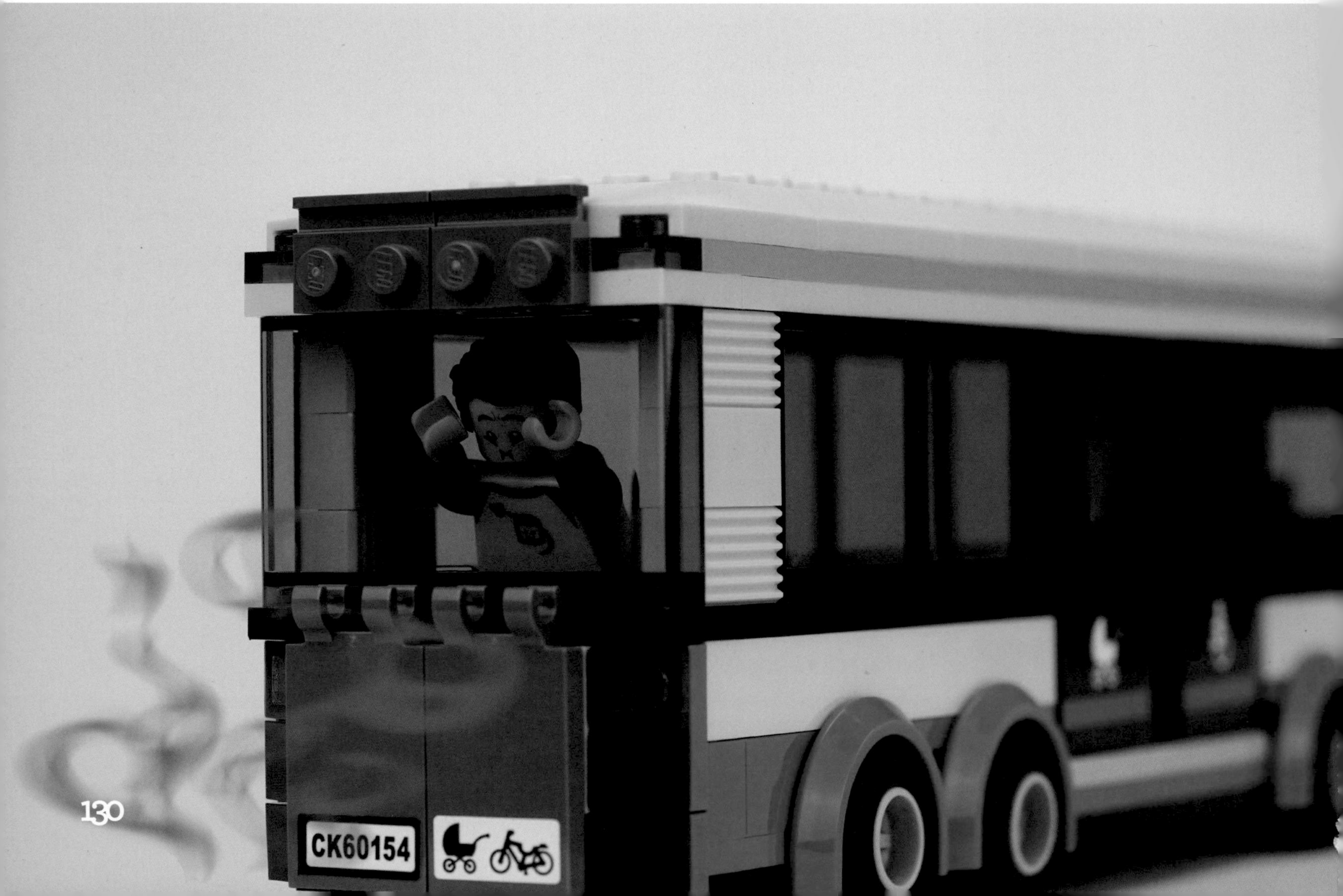
CK60154

Britain's first "poo bus," which runs on human and household waste, commenced regular services in Bristol, UK in March 2015.

The Bio-Bus (as it is properly known) was operated by bus company First West of England, with a schedule of four days per week from March 2015. During its fifteen-mile route, the Bio-Bus uses waste from more than 32,000 households! The bus will fill up at a site in Bristol, where sewage and food waste are turned into biomethane gas. The Bio-Bus was first unveiled in Bristol in 2014 and has been introduced as a regular fixture due to worldwide attention. Managing Director of First West James Freeman says more "poo buses" will be introduced if the scheme is successful.

ROBOTS TEACH ENGLISH TO SOUTH KOREANS

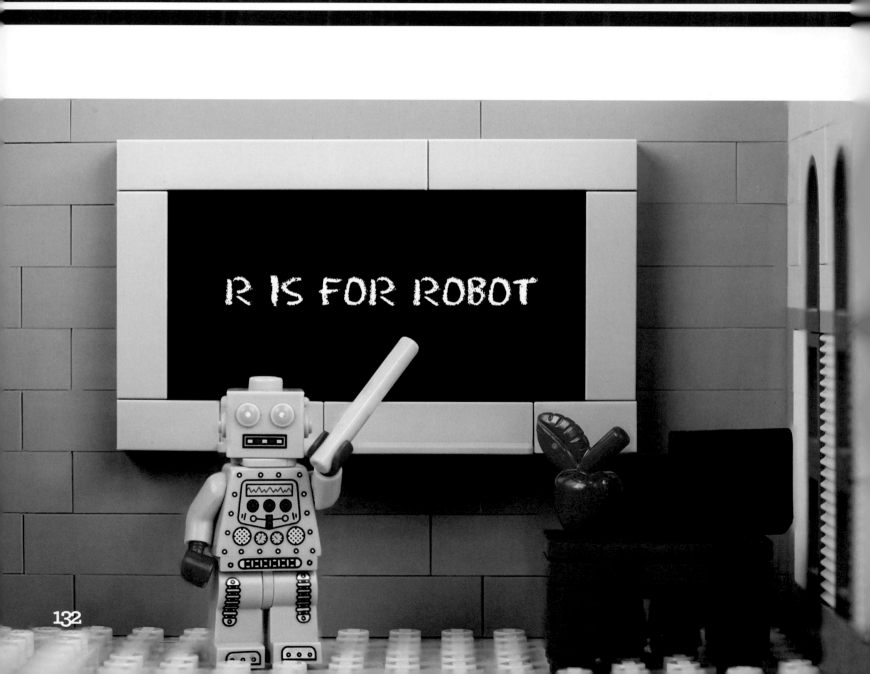

The South Korean government launched a pilot program for two classrooms in the city of Masan, whereby students would be taught English by a robot, Engkey.

Engkey is controlled remotely by a human teacher outside of the classroom, whose face appears on the screen. According to a senior researcher at the Korea Institute of Science and Technology, the educational robot system "helps increase students' interest and self-motivation in studying English and improves their English skills." The robot learning (or "R-learning") program also serves to introduce teachers and types of learning otherwise not available in a cost-effective manner, with teachers as far as Australia offering remote assistance. The plan is to introduce more robots in the coming years.

SWEDISH LAB DEVELOPS SPIDER SILK

Thanks to scientists in Sweden, your dream of shooting spider webs like Spider-Man could become reality!

Scientists at the Swedish University of Agricultural Sciences and Karolinska Institute say they have developed a technique to create artificial spider silk from bacteria, possibly in large quantities! Spider silk is as strong as steel, yet incredibly flexible. The science talk? Spidroin genes from two spider species are combined, with the resulting hybrid silk protein then inserted into the DNA of bacteria. When this is put to use in a newly designed spinning device—BAM, synthetic spider silk! It's believed that the silk could be used for tissue engineering applications, but we all know what it could really be used for. The future is now!

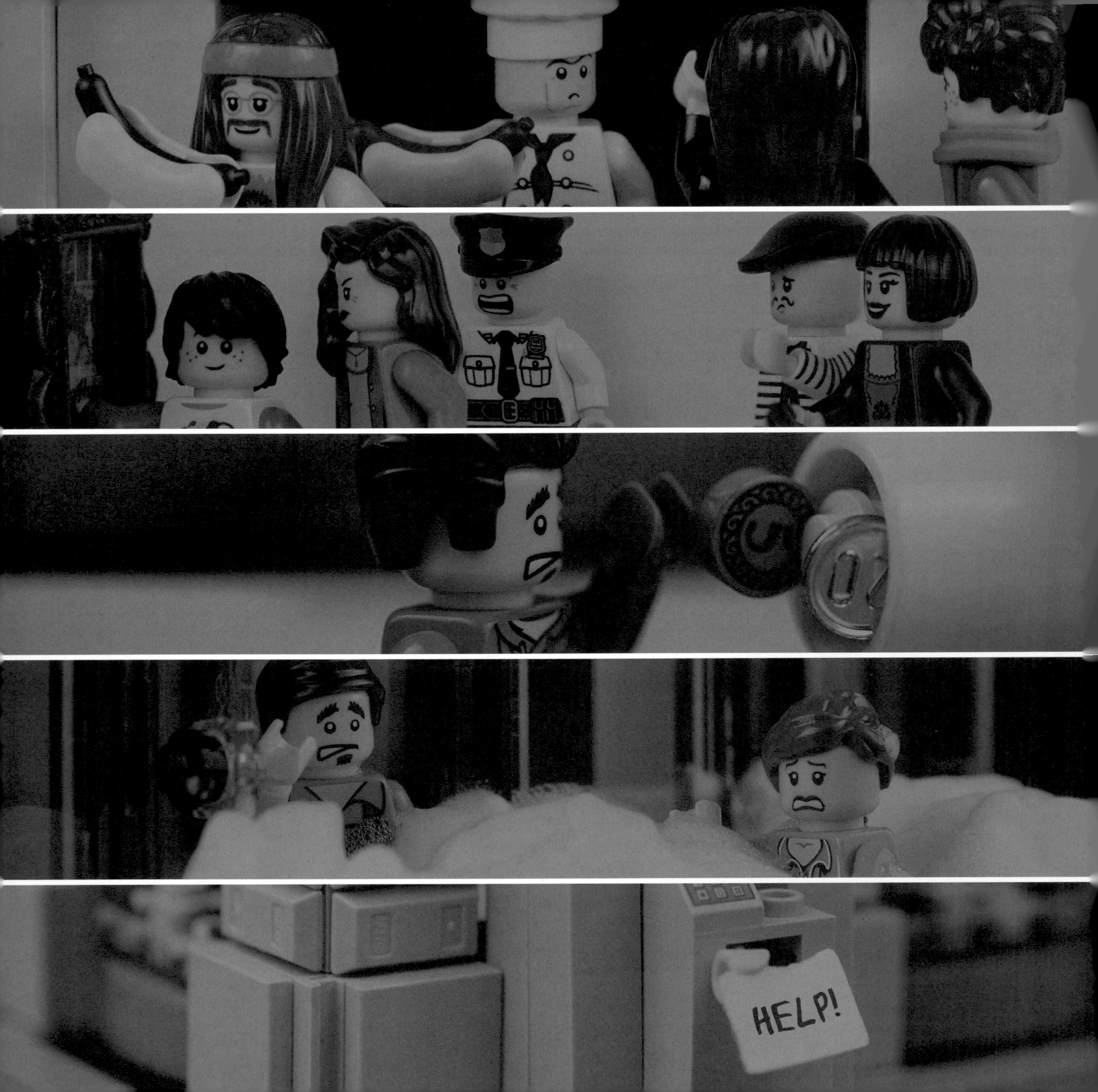
HELP!

CHAPTER 8

OOPS!

REPAIRMAN STUCK IN ATM USES NOTE DISPENSER TO PLEAD FOR HELP

A repairman got stuck inside an ATM in Corpus Christi, Texas, so he used the receipt slot to dispense notes asking for help!

The man was sent to repair a door lock in the room that contained the ATM, but forgot to bring a device used to open the door from the inside and his mobile phone. The man's note read: "Please help. I'm stuck in here, and I don't have my phone. Please call my boss," with the number below. Officer Richard Olden said he could hear "a little voice" coming from the ATM after he was waved down by locals who had received the man's note along with their transaction. Police kicked down the door to release the man and thankfully no harm came to any money.

BOY TRIPS AND PUNCHES HOLE IN MILLION-DOLLAR PAINTING!

A twelve-year-old boy accidentally tripped and punched a hole in a 350-year-old Italian painting worth $1.5 million while it was on exhibit in Taiwan.

"Flowers" by Italian master Paolo Porpora was one of fifty-five pieces at the *Faces of Leonardo* exhibition in Taipei. Video footage showed that the boy was listening to the guide when he lost his balance and stumbled over the safety rope before pressing a soda can into the painting. It's reported that the boy and his family expressed sincere regret for the incident and the organizers did not seek damages from the boy's parents for the painting, which was promptly restored. The child is lucky—a Leonardo da Vinci self-portrait (worth $231 million) was also on display.

MYTHBUSTERS CANNONBALL EXPERIMENT GOES WRONG

A cannonball fired during a Mythbusters stunt missed its intended target, and instead rolled 700 yards through a Californian neighborhood, smashed through the front door of a home, then upstairs past the owners as they slept, before eventually crashing into a parked car.

The Mythbusters team used a bomb disposal range in Dublin, California to test whether other materials could be fired out of a cannon. In this case, the cannonball was supposed to pierce a wall after moving through trash cans filled with water, but the path of destruction indicates that something did not go to plan. According to Alameda County Sherriff's Department, the incident in Dublin, California was "crazy, crazy, crazy." Thankfully, nobody was hurt by the cannonball, which was travelling at 1,000 feet per second!

STOLEN SUBARU RETURNED WITH GAS MONEY AND NOTE

A Subaru was accidentally "stolen" from a woman and then returned the next night with gas money and a nice note explaining the mix-up.

As the story goes, a woman gave her friend a key and instructions to collect the woman's red Subaru from a Portland neighborhood. The friend returned with a red Subaru, but this one belonged to another woman from the same neighborhood. Unfortunately for everyone involved, Subaru keys are said to be somewhat interchangeable. The owner of the stolen Subaru reported it as stolen, with the footage revealing a (naturally) very casual theft, but the car was returned the next night with $30 and a note from the woman explaining that she did not realize her friend had collected the wrong car until the next morning.

ITALIAN VALET DESTROYS FERRARI AFTER MISTAKING ACCELERATOR FOR BRAKE!

An Italian valet destroyed a $450,000 2012 Ferrari GTO 599 after he mistook the accelerator for the brake.

According to *Corriere della Sera*, Roberto Cinti told police he got confused and accidentally pressed the accelerator instead of the brake. Roberto also destroyed the Orietta Astrologo shopfront, leaving only the "Ori" part of the trading name on the sign visible. It's reported that Roberto was delivering the car to its Dutch owners, who had taken part in a Ferrari Owner's Club meeting. Roberto was taken to hospital for treatment of mild injuries and shock. The 2012 Ferrari GTO 599 can go from zero to sixty miles per hour in three seconds, and can reach speeds of up to 200 miles per hour.

FRENCH ROADSIDE CAFÉ ACCIDENTALLY AWARDED MICHELIN STAR

A roadside café in France was inundated with customers after it was confused with an upscale restaurant and accidentally awarded a Michelin star!

Le Bouche à Oreille (which means "word of mouth") in Bourges central France, was included on a map of starred restaurants published by Michelin. The cafe is a lunch only bistro serviced by a part-time chef and the owner, who runs between the bar and tables, with meals (including a jug of wine!) costing about $15. However, the star was meant to go an upscale restaurant of the same name in Boutervilliers, southwest of Paris, with the streets being similarly named as well!

The error was taken in good spirits, with the restaurant owners inviting each other over to try their specialties.

FLIGHT DELAYED DUE TO COINS THROWN INTO ENGINE

A plane had to be evacuated for several hours after an elderly passenger threw coins into the engine for good luck!

It's reported that the eighty-year-old woman "prayed for safety," then threw nine coins at the engine as she crossed the tarmac to enter the plane. Although only one coin reached the engine, it was enough to cause an evacuation of the China Southern Airlines plane at the Shanghai Sudong International Airport. It's believed that authorities were alerted to the "strange behavior" by another passenger. The woman and her family were taken into custody for questioning, but later released without charge. Police say they recovered coins to the value of approximately 1.7 yuan ($0.25).

NOT EVERYONE "GETS" MODERN ART...

Cleaners at the Museion art gallery in Bolzano, Italy threw an art installation in the bin, believing it to be rubbish left over from a party!

The avant-garde exhibition by Milan artists Sara Goldschmied and Eleonora Chiari was titled "Dove andiamo a ballare questa sera" ("Where are we going to dance tonight?"). Intended as a commentary on Italy's "Age of Plenty" in the 1980s, the artists scattered empty champagne bottles, cigarette butts, confetti, shoes, and clothing on the floor to symbolize the mess that follows a party. However, when cleaning staff arrived at the gallery, they mistook the modern art for actual leftovers from a party the night before and threw the items into bin or recycling bags.

Thankfully the artwork was soon salvaged and reinstalled at the gallery.

REALITY TV CONTESTANTS SPEND ONE YEAR ABROAD BUT NOBODY IS WATCHING

154

Contestants in a year-long reality TV social experiment returned home to find out that the show was pulled from the air after four months due to bad ratings.

The premise of *Eden* is that twenty-three strangers were sent to the Highlands in Scotland to build a self-sufficient community without the use of modern technology or equipment. Filming on the Channel 4 program started in March 2016, with thirteen contestants ultimately dropping out during the year due to infighting and hunger. Upon their return, the remaining contestants are reported to have said that they "were not informed that their ordeal had not been broadcast since August [2016]." Channel 4 aired the final five episodes of the show in August 2017.

THE DAY FOAM TOOK OVER SANTA CLARA

The Californian town of Santa Clara was taken over by foam following the accidental discharge of fire retardant at San Jose Airport!

It's reported that the San Jose Fire Department arrived to find a three-meter foam blob that almost covered street signs, but no fire. Captain Mitch Matlow said the foam can be carcinogenic in high concentration, which may have worried a cyclist who looked to be having a great time in the foam, which he said felt and smelled like soap. The foam is an aqueous film forming foam, which was invented by Russian engineer Aleksandr Loran in 1902. The film works by cooling the fire and coating fuel so it does not come into further contact with oxygen.

THE SHORT NEWS

MAKING THE NEWS FUN SINCE JUNE 2014

The Short News is not like any other news site in the world. Sure, there are words, but each picture contains toys instead of real life people, animals and things. These toys are used to give life to funny, offbeat, and light-hearted news stories from around the world.

Yes, the stories are all real (this is a common question), and they are carefully selected to educate and entertain people of all ages. Each story is represented by a unique image, which is accompanied by a concise caption.

The Short News shoots with Sony, in a very crowded studio located in Victoria, Australia.

You can follow The Short News at:

http://theshortnews.com/

Instagram: @theshortnews

Facebook: @theshortnewz

Twitter: @theshortnewz